Multilevel Activity Book

SERIES DIRECTOR
Jayme Adelson-Goldstein

Jill Korey O'Sullivan

OXFORD
UNIVERSITY PRESS

OXFORD
UNIVERSITY PRESS

198 Madison Avenue
New York, NY 10016 USA

Great Clarendon Street, Oxford OX2 6DP UK

Oxford University Press is a department of the University of Oxford.
It furthers the University's objective of excellence in research, scholarship,
and education by publishing worldwide in

Oxford New York

Auckland Cape Town Dar es Salaam Hong Kong Karachi
Kuala Lumpur Madrid Melbourne Mexico City Nairobi
New Delhi Shanghai Taipei Toronto

With offices in

Argentina Austria Brazil Chile Czech Republic France Greece
Guatemala Hungary Italy Japan Poland Portugal Singapore
South Korea Switzerland Thailand Turkey Ukraine Vietnam

OXFORD and OXFORD ENGLISH are registered trademarks of
Oxford University Press

Executive Publisher: Janet Aitchison
Editorial Manager: Stephanie Karras
Senior Editor: Sharon Sargent
Art Director: Maj-Britt Hagsted
Senior Designer: Claudia Carlson
Art Editor: Robin Fadool
Production Manager: Shanta Persaud
Production Controller: Eve Wong

Printed in Hong Kong

10 9 8 7 6 5 4 3 2 1

ISBN-13: 978 0 19 4398268

ISBN-10: 0 19 4398269

Acknowledgements

Illustrations by: Laurie Conley, p.18, p.19, p.50, p.88, p.89, 130; John Batten,
p.20, p.40, p.70, p.108, p.109; Michael Hortens, p.26, p.56, p.96, p.116;
Geo Parkin, p.28, p.29, p.48, p.49, p.100, p.128, p.129; Bill Dickson, p.30,
p.80, p.98, p.99, p.110, p.120; Arlene Boehm, p.36, p.76, p.126, p.136;
Shawn Banner, p.38, p.39, p.78, p.79, p.90; Annie Bissett, p.46, p.106;
Kevin Brown, p.68, p.69; p.118, p.119.

We would like to thank the following for their permission to reproduce photographs
Dennis Kitchen, p.1.

I would like to thank the editorial and production
staff at Oxford University Press for all of the hard
work they put into the creation of this book.
Thanks especially to Amy Cooper for her creative,
insightful and meticulous editing, and to Sharon
Sargent and Jayme Adelson-Goldstein for their
guidance throughout the writing of the book.

This one's for mom.

Jill Korey O'Sullivan

Kudos to the amazing *Multilevel Activity Book 3*
team members who performed their assigned roles
with panache: Jill Korey—inspired writer;
Amy Cooper—gifted facilitator; Maj-Britt Hagsted,
Claudia Carlson and Niki Barolini—artful designers;
Robin Fadool—resourceful picture finder; and
Sharon Sargent, Stephanie Karras and Janet Aitchison—
expert timekeepers and question askers.

To Amy, xox

Jayme Adelson-Goldstein

Acknowledgments

The Publisher and Series Director would like to acknowledge the following individuals for their invaluable input during the development of this series:

Vittoria Abbatte-Maghsoudi Mount Diablo Unified School District, Loma Vista Adult Center, Concord, CA

Karen Abell Durham Technical Community College, Durham, NC

Millicent Alexander Los Angeles Unified School District, Huntington Park-Bell Community Adult School, Los Angeles, CA

Diana Allen Oakton Community College, Skokie, IL

Bethany Bandera Arlington Education and Employment Program, Arlington, VA

Sandra Bergman New York City Department of Education, New York, NY

Chan Bostwick Los Angeles Technology Center, Los Angeles, CA

Diana Brady-Herndon Napa Valley Adult School, Napa, CA

Susan Burlos Baldwin Park Unified School District, Baldwin Park, CA

Carmen Carbajal Mitchell Community College, Statesville, NC

Jose Carmona Daytona Beach Community College, Daytona Beach, FL

Ingrid Caswell Los Angeles Technology Center, Los Angeles, CA

Joyce Clapp Hayward Adult School, Hayward, CA

Beverly deNicola Capistrano Unified School District, San Juan Capistrano, CA

Edward Ende Miami Springs Adult Center, Miami Springs, FL

Gayle Fagan Harris County Department of Education, Houston, TX

Richard Firsten Lindsey Hopkins Technical Education Center, Miami, FL

Elizabeth Fitzgerald Hialeah Adult Center, Hialeah, FL

Mary Ann Florez Arlington Education and Employment Program, Arlington, VA

Leslie Foster Davidson Mitchell Community College, Statesville, NC

Beverly Gandall Santa Ana College School of Continuing Education, Santa Ana, CA

Rodriguez Garner Westchester Community College, Valhalla, NY

Sally Gearhart Santa Rosa Junior College, Santa Rosa, CA

Norma Guzman Baldwin Park Unified School District, Baldwin Park, CA

Lori Howard UC Berkeley, Education Extension, Berkeley, CA

Phillip L. Johnson Santa Ana College Centennial Education Center, Santa Ana, CA

Kelley Keith Mount Diablo Unified School District, Loma Vista Adult Center, Concord, CA

Blanche Kellawon Bronx Community College, Bronx, NY

Keiko Kimura Triton College, River Grove, IL

Jody Kirkwood ABC Adult School, Cerritos, CA

Matthew Kogan Evans Community Adult School, Los Angeles, CA

Laurel Leonard Napa Valley Adult School, Napa, CA

Barbara Linek Illinois Migrant Education Council, Plainfield, IL

Alice Macondray Neighborhood Centers Adult School, Oakland, CA

Ronna Magy Los Angeles Unified School District Central Office, Los Angeles, CA

Jose Marlasca South Area Adult Education, Melbourne, FL

Laura Martin Adult Learning Resource Center, Des Plaines, IL

Judith Martin-Hall Indian River Community College, Fort Pierce, FL

Michael Mason Mount Diablo Unified School District, Loma Vista Adult Center, Concord, CA

Katherine McCaffery Brewster Technical Center, Tampa, FL

Cathleen McCargo Arlington Education and Employment Program, Arlington, VA

Todd McDonald Hillsborough County Public Schools, Tampa, FL

Rita McSorley Northeast Independent School District, San Antonio, TX

Gloria Melendrez Evans Community Adult School, Los Angeles, CA

Vicki Moore El Monte-Rosemead Adult School, El Monte, CA

Meg Morris Mountain View Los Altos Adult Education District, Los Altos, CA

Nieves Novoa LaGuardia Community College, Long Island City, NY

Jo Pamment Haslett Public Schools, East Lansing, MI

Liliana Quijada-Black Irvington Learning Center, Houston, TX

Ellen Quish LaGuardia Community College, Long Island City, NY

Mary Ray Fairfax County Public Schools, Springfield, VA

Tatiana Roganova Hayward Adult School, Hayward, CA

Nancy Rogenscky-Roda Hialeah-Miami Lakes Adult Education and Community Center, Hialeah, FL

Lorraine Romero Houston Community College, Houston, TX

Edilyn Samways The English Center, Miami, FL

Kathy Santopietro Weddel Northern Colorado Literacy Program, Littleton, CO

Dr. G. Santos The English Center, Miami, FL

Fran Schnall City College of New York Literacy Program, New York, NY

Mary Segovia El Monte-Rosemead Adult School, El Monte, CA

Edith Smith City College of San Francisco, San Francisco, CA

Alisa Takeuchi Chapman Education Center Garden Grove, CA

Leslie Weaver Fairfax County Public Schools, Falls Church, VA

David Wexler Napa Valley Adult School, Napa, CA

Bartley P. Wilson Northeast Independent School District, San Antonio, TX

Emily Wonson Hunter College, New York, NY

Contents

Unit 10 Crime Doesn't Pay

Unit 11 That's Life

Unit 12 Do the Right Thing

Introduction to the *Step Forward Multilevel Activity Book 3*

Welcome to the *Step Forward Multilevel Activity Book 3*. In these pages you'll find a wealth of highly interactive activities that require little preparation. All of the activities can be used in numerous ways with a variety of learners. The activities in this book are effective in intermediate classes as well as in multilevel classes with learners ranging from low-beginning to high-intermediate levels.

This book is divided into 12 units that directly correspond to *Step Forward Student Book 3*. Each activity supports and expands upon the student book's lesson objectives, for a complete approach to English language learning.

1 What is the Multilevel Activity Book?

The *Multilevel Activity Book 3* (like the entire *Step Forward* series) is based on research that says adults taught in a learner-centered classroom retain more material for longer periods of time (McCombs and Whistler 1997, Benson and Voller 1997). Through its guided and communicative practice opportunities, the *Multilevel Activity Book 3* provides hours of meaningful and fun classroom activities.

2 How do I use these reproducible activities?

The Teaching Notes on pages 3–11 give detailed directions on how to conduct each activity and also provide multilevel suggestions. They guide you through

1. setting up the activity,
2. modeling/demonstrating the activity,
3. checking your learners' comprehension of each activity's goal and directions.

Once learners understand how to proceed, they are able to work together to complete the activities. Putting learning into the learners' hands is an important step towards ensuring that they will achieve the lesson objective. Moving away from the front-and-center role frees you to circulate, monitor, facilitate, and gain insight into how well the lesson information was captured. You discover what learners can and can't do well, and adjust your future lesson plans accordingly.

3 What makes these activities multilevel?

One of the key techniques in multilevel instruction is to use materials that can work across levels. There are eight activity types in this book. Each one allows you to target practice to the learner's abilities, but still have the entire class working on the same basic activity. (See the photo below for an example.) Having only eight activity types means that students quickly understand how to do the activities, requiring less teacher intervention and more learner-directed

The Jigsaw Readings in *Multilevel Activity Book 3* allow learners to work at their own level and pace. Higher-level pairs use more complex language to talk about the readings while lower-level pairs use simpler language to perform the same task.

practice. Each activity includes a Keep Going suggestion for a follow-up activity, such as discussing answers, sharing opinions about a related topic or reporting on a task. The eight activity types are described below.

ACTIVITY	GROUPING STRATEGY	DESCRIPTION	CORRELATION TO *Step Forward Student Book 3*
Mixer	Whole Class	Learners get acquainted as they ask and answer questions.	**Pre-unit: The First Step**
Picture Differences	Pairs	Learners reinforce their understanding of target words and phrases by identifying differences between two pictures.	**Lesson 1: Vocabulary**
Round Table Writing	Small groups	Learners take turns writing sentences about a picture.	**Lesson 2: Real-life writing**
Peer Dictation	Pairs	Partners take turns dictating sentences that reinforce grammar structures while developing their clarification strategies.	**Lesson 3: Grammar**
Survey	Whole Class; Pairs	Learners gather classmates' information and write sentences about the results.	**Lesson 3: Grammar**
Role-Play	Small Groups	Learners develop fluency by practicing and expanding upon conversation gambits.	**Lesson 4: Everyday conversation**
Jigsaw Reading	Pairs	Partners read a high-interest text and answer questions. They then work with another pair to learn about that pair's reading and answer questions about their own.	**Lesson 5: Real-life reading**
Team Project	Small Groups	Learners work together to complete a project.	**Review and expand**

By having pairs or small groups practice the language required to meet a lesson objective, teachers facilitate learners' use and internalization of the target language. This also provides important opportunities for learners to engage in real-life interaction strategies such as negotiating meaning, checking information, disagreeing, and reaching consensus.

While a pair of running shoes is not required equipment, most multilevel instructors find themselves on the move in the classroom.

These highly structured activities support the energetic, communicative, and lively approach to learning that is the hallmark of effective multilevel instruction. The Step Forward Team hopes that you and your learners enjoy these activities.

Please write to us with your comments and questions: **Stepforwardteam.us@oup.com.**

Jayme Adelson-Goldstein

Jayme Adelson-Goldstein, Series Director

Multilevel Activity Teaching Notes

Teaching Notes for the Mixer

Focus: Students get to know each other by asking and answering questions.
Grouping Strategy: Whole class
Activity Time: 25–30 minutes
Student Book Connection: Pre-unit The First Step

Ready,

1. Select a Mixer activity.

2. Duplicate one activity page for each student.

3. Write the question(s) from Step 1 of the Mixer on the board.

Set...

1. Share the goal of the activity: *You're going to talk to your classmates to learn more about each other.*

2. Have a higher-level volunteer ask the question(s) on the board.

3. Elicit responses to the question(s) on the board from the class.

4. Distribute an activity page to each student and review the directions.

5. As indicated in the directions, ask students to add one or more questions of their own.

6. Ask two volunteers to come to the front and model the activity, using the first Mixer question.

7. Check students' comprehension by asking *yes/no* questions. *Do you answer the questions yourself?* [no]

Go!

1. Set a time limit (five minutes).

2. Have students circulate to complete the activity page. Tell them to sit down when their activity page is complete and have them write sentences about their classmates, using the information from the survey.

3. Give students a two-minute warning.

4. Call "time."

Keep Going!

Have students complete the Keep Going activity on the Mixer page.

Multilevel Suggestions

Before the Activity:

Pre-Level: Help students read the questions and write their own answers in their notebooks. Pair each pre-level student with a higher-level student. Have the partners work together to write the additional question(s).

On-Level: Have students read the questions and write their answers in their notebooks. Have students write the additional question(s) independently.

Higher-Level: Have students write the additional question(s) independently, and then help the pre-level students write their question(s).

Teaching Notes for the Picture Differences

Focus: Students work together to find ten differences between two pictures.
Grouping Strategy: Pairs
Activity Time: 20–25 minutes
Student Book Connection: Lesson 1

Ready,

1. Select the Picture Differences activity that corresponds to the unit you are teaching in *Step Forward Student Book 3.*

2. Duplicate one set of activity pages for each pair of students.

3. Check the picture differences yourself to determine what, if any, new vocabulary students will need in order to communicate the differences. Introduce new vocabulary as needed.

4. Draw a simple picture on the left side of the board (such as a stick figure). Draw the picture again on the right side of the board, this time with one difference (such as the stick figure wearing a hat). Ask students to identify the difference between the two pictures and to describe the pictures in sentence form. Write the students' sentences under the pictures. Picture A: *The man isn't wearing a hat.* Picture B: *The man is wearing a hat.*

Set...

1. Share the goal of the activity: *You're going to work together to find the differences between your pictures. This will help you practice vocabulary.*

2. Have two volunteers demonstrate the activity.
 • Identify one student as Partner A and the other as Partner B.
 • Give Picture A to Partner A and give Picture B to Partner B.
 • Have the partners work together to examine the two pictures and find a difference between them.
 • Have the partners work together to write two sentences that describe the picture difference that they found.

3. Pair students, assign *A/B* roles, and distribute one set of activity pages to each pair.

4. Review the directions.

5. Check comprehension by asking pre-level students *yes/no* questions: *Do you show your partner your picture?* [yes] Ask on-level and higher-level students information questions: *How many differences should you find?* [10]

Go!

1. Set a time limit (ten minutes).

2. A/B pairs work together, identifying the picture differences and writing sentences to describe these differences. Students continue until they've identified ten differences between the pictures and written two sentences for each difference (a total of twenty sentences).

3. Monitor progress and assist students as needed.

4. Call "time." Have volunteers write their sentences on the board and then have the class correct spelling as needed.

Keep Going!

Have students talk about a picture-related topic, using the discussion prompt on the activity page.

Multilevel Suggestions

For Mixed-Level Pairs:
Instruct pre-level students to say or circle the differences they find. Have on-level and higher-level students write the sentences their pre-level partner expresses.

For Same-Level Pairs:
Pre-Level: Before pre-level students begin the activity, review the key vocabulary for the items in the pictures. Allow pre-level students to express differences with sentence fragments rather than full sentences.

On-Level: Have students complete the activity as outlined above.

Higher-Level: Have higher-level students write 5–10 sentences about things that are the same in the pictures.

Teaching Notes for the Round Table Writing

Focus: Students study a picture and then take turns writing sentences about it.
Grouping Strategy: Groups of 4 students
Activity Time: 20–30 minutes
Student Book Connection: Lesson 2

Ready,

1. Select the Round Table Writing activity that corresponds to the unit you are teaching in *Step Forward Student Book 3*.

2. Duplicate one activity page for every four students.

3. On the board, draw a simple picture and write a sample sentence that could be the first line in a story about the picture.

4. Provide a review of the vocabulary and concepts represented in the Round Table Writing picture.

Set...

1. Share the goal of the activity: *You're going to work together to look at a picture, and then take turns writing sentences about it.*

2. Form groups of four students.

3. Model the activity, using the picture and the sample sentence on the board. Ask a volunteer to form another sentence based on the picture. Write the volunteer's sentence on the board, following the sample sentence.

4. Distribute one activity page to each group and review the directions.

5. Check comprehension by asking *yes/no* questions. *Do you write all of the sentences yourself?* [no] *Should all of the sentences be about the picture?* [yes]

6. Have students, in their groups, read the sample sentence silently as you read it aloud.

Go!

1. Set a time limit (fifteen minutes).

2. Students take turns, each writing one sentence and then passing the sheet to another group member. Students continue to take turns until they've written as many sentences as they can within the time limit.

2. Monitor the groups' progress. Assist students as needed.

3. Once a group is finished writing, have them read through their sentences, identify the words they're unsure of, and assign each group member one or more words to check in the dictionary.

4. Call "time."

Keep Going!

Have each group choose a Reporter to read their three most interesting sentences to another group. Then the Reporter travels to another group to read the sentences. Repeat this reporting process at least twice.

Multilevel Suggestions

For Mixed-Level Groups:
Tell pre-level students they can say rather than write the sentences. Instruct on-level and higher-level students to write their pre-level group members' ideas on the activity page and to make sure the sentences are grammatically correct.

For Same-Level Groups:
Pre-Level: Review and write on the board the vocabulary that students will need in order to complete the activity. You may also wish to ask students *yes/no* questions about the picture. Such questions will help students construct their own sentences.

On-Level: Have students complete the activity as outlined above.

Higher-Level: Before assigning the activity to these students, provide several prompts that will encourage students to write sentences based on their ideas and opinions. For example, *Have you ever been in this situation? What is your opinion of what the man is doing? If you were in this situation, what would you do?*

Teaching Notes for the Peer Dictation

Focus: Students dictate sentences to each other to complete the activity page.
Grouping Strategy: Pairs
Activity Time: 15-25 minutes
Student Book Connection: Lesson 3

Ready,

1. Select the Peer Dictation activity that corresponds to the unit you are teaching in *Step Forward Student Book 3*.

2. Duplicate one activity page for each student.

3. On the left side of the board, write a sentence that relates to the topic. Label this side of the board *Partner A*. Label the right side of the board *Partner B*.

4. Familiarize students with the dictation process by asking volunteers to read the sentence on the left side of the board to you. Before you write the sentence on the board, repeat it back, incorrectly. Encourage students to correct you by reading the sentence to you again. Next, repeat the sentence correctly, and write it on the right side of the board.

Set...

1. Share the goal of the activity: *You're going to practice reading, listening to, and writing sentences.*

2. Have one volunteer pair model the activity for the class. Ask the pair to come to the front and sit across from each other. Give each partner one of the activity pages. Tell the partners what to do as the class watches and listens.
  • *Fold your papers.*
  • *Partner A, look at the top. Partner B, look at the bottom.*
  • *Partner A, read the first sentence on the page to your partner.*
  • *Partner B, repeat what you hear.*
  • *Partner A, confirm that Partner B heard the sentence correctly.*
  • *Partner B, write the sentence.*

3. When A finishes, have B dictate the first sentence on the bottom half of the sheet to A.

4. Distribute one activity page per person and review the directions.

5. Pair students, assign *A/B* roles, and have them fold their activity pages.

6. Check comprehension by asking *or* questions. *Do you fold or cut the paper?* [fold] *Does Partner A read the A sentences or the B sentences?* [the A sentences]

Go!

1. Set a time limit (five minutes) for A to dictate to B.

2. Call "time" and set a time limit (five minutes) for B to dictate to A.

3. Call "time" and have pairs unfold their papers and check their work.

Keep Going!

Have students each write five sentences on the topic suggested in the prompt. Point out the example sentence, and encourage students to use the target grammar. Have students talk about their sentences with a partner. Have each pair dictate one of their sentences to the class.

Multilevel Suggestions

For Mixed-Level Pairs:
Pair on-level or higher-level students with pre-level students. Allow pre-level students to either write or to dictate, depending on what they would rather do.

For Same-Level Pairs:
Pre-Level: Provide a simplified version of the peer dictation by covering all but a key word or phrase in each sentence on the activity page and then duplicating it for the students. Conduct the activity as outlined above.

On-Level: Have students complete the activity as outlined above.

Higher-Level: Review the information question words: *who, what, where, when*. Direct students to purposely obscure one of the words in each sentence as they dictate. This will force their partner to clarify before they write. For example, Partner A: *Yesterday, Carlos went to the* [mumble: *library*]. Partner B: *Where did Carlos go?*

Teaching Notes for the Survey

Focus: Students conduct a survey and then write sentences about the results.
Grouping Strategy: Whole class, Pairs
Activity Time: 30–40 minutes
Student Book Connection: Lesson 3

Ready,

1. Select the Survey activity that corresponds to the unit you are teaching in *Step Forward Student Book 3*.

2. Duplicate one activity page for each student.

3. Draw a simplified chart on the board based on the first row of the survey chart.

4. Ask the first survey question and answer it yourself. Put your answer under the "My answers" column of the chart.

5. Ask three students the same question, and fill in their responses on the chart.

Set...

1. Share the goal of the activity: *You're going to ask and answer questions about ____ with your classmates. Then you're going to work with a partner. You will compare your classmates' answers and write sentences about them.*

2. Distribute one activity page per person and review the directions. Check comprehension by asking information questions. *Who answers each question first?* [I do.] *How many other students do you interview for each question?* [three]

3. Have students silently read and respond to the survey questions, marking their responses in the column titled "My answers."

4. Set a time limit (ten minutes).

Go!

1. Direct students to interview three other students and to write the responses of those students in the chart.

2. Set a time limit (10 minutes).

3. Circulate and monitor students' progress.

4. Call "time."

5. Have students sit with a partner to compare their charts and write sentences about their comparison. Set a time limit (5 minutes).

6. Assist students as needed.

Keep Going!

Have students talk about the topic using the discussion prompt on the activity page.

Multilevel Suggestions

For Mixed-Level Groups:
To help pre-level students fully participate in the survey, duplicate the activity page in three colors. Distribute one color to pre-level students, one color to on-level students, and one to higher-level students. Tell students they can only survey students with a different color paper.

For Same-Level Groups:
Pre-Level: Students can answer questions with single words or sentence fragments.

On-Level: Have students complete the activity as outlined above. Encourage students to use the target grammar in their responses.

Higher-Level: Encourage students to ask each other two or three follow-up questions.

Teaching Notes for the Role Play

Focus: Working in groups, students read, choose roles, write the ending, and act out a role-play.
Grouping Strategy: Groups of 3-4 students.
Activity Time: 45–60 minutes
Student Book Connection: Lesson 4

Ready,

1. Select the Role Play activity that corresponds to the unit you are teaching in *Step Forward Student Book 3*.

2. Duplicate one activity page for each student.

3. Check the "Props" list to determine what items you need to bring to class. You will need one set of props for every two-to-three students.

4. Check the script to determine what, if any, new vocabulary students will need in order to do the role-play.

Set...

1. Share the goal of the activity: *You're going to work in groups and act out different parts in a role-play.*

2. Have students form groups according to the number of characters.

3. Distribute one activity page per person and one set of props per group. Review the directions: *First read the script. Next decide who will play each character. Then write an ending. You must add more lines for each character.*

4. Present new vocabulary or review vocabulary as needed.

5. Check comprehension by asking *yes/no* questions. *Do you say all the lines?* [no] *Do you act out your lines?* [yes]

6. Invite two volunteers to the front. Have each pick a line of dialog from the script and act it out for the class.

Go!

1. Set a time limit (fifteen minutes) for the group to read the script, choose their characters, and finish the role-play.

2. Set a time limit (five minutes) and have the students act out the role-play in their groups.

3. Monitor student's progress by walking around and helping with problems such as register or pronunciation (rhythm, stress, and intonation). Encourage pantomime and improvisation.

Keep Going!

Have each group perform their role-play for the class. Ask students, while watching the role-plays, to write the answers to the questions in the Keep Going section on the activity page.

Multilevel Suggestions

For Mixed-Level Groups:
Adapt the role-play to include a non-speaking or limited speaking role for pre-level students who are not ready to participate verbally. For example, add a character who only answers *yes* or *no* to questions asked by another character. In larger classes, you may want to assign a higher-level student as a "director" for each group.

For Same-Level Groups:
Pre-Level: On the board, write a simplified conversation based on the role-play situation. Help students read and copy the conversation in their notebooks. Then have pairs practice the conversation until they can perform it without the script.

On-Level: Have students complete the activity as outlined above.

Higher-Level: Have students create their own version of the role-play using related vocabulary or a similar situation.

Teaching Notes for the Jigsaw Reading

Focus: Students read a text and exchange information with another pair who read a complimentary text.
Grouping Strategy: Pairs
Activity Time: 30–40 minutes
Student Book Connection: Lesson 5

Ready,

1. Select the Jigsaw Readings that correspond to the unit you are teaching in *Step Forward Student Book 3.*

2. Duplicate one set of activity pages for every four students. Using different color paper for the A and B articles makes it easier to group students.

3. Model the general concept of the Jigsaw Reading by doing the following: Ask four volunteers to turn their backs to the board. Label the left side of the board *Pair A.* Write a simple sentence on this side, such as *Mark lives in Chicago.* Label the right side of the board *Pair B.* On this side, write a question relating to Pair A's sentence, such as *Where does Mark live?* Lead two volunteers to each side of the board, telling them to read silently only what is on their side. Ask Pair B to ask their question. Prompt Pair A to answer with the information from their sentence. Ask B to write the answer below the question on the board. You may wish to repeat this process with a Pair B "reading" and a Pair A question. *Pair B: Alma works in a restaurant. Pair A: What does Alma do?*

Set...

1. Share the goal of the activity: *You're going to practice reading, and then asking and answering questions about what you read.*

2. Present new vocabulary or review vocabulary as needed.

3. Have half the students seated on one side of the room pair up as "A" partners. Have students on the other side of the room pair up as "B" partners. Distribute the A activity pages to each member of the A pairs, and the B activity pages to each member of the B pairs.

4. Review the directions for Steps 1, 2, and 3.

5. Check comprehension by asking *yes/no* questions. *Do you read both articles?* [no] *Do you ask questions about your partner's article?* [yes]

Go!

1. Set a time limit (five minutes) for the students to read their text. Observe students during silent reading, and assist any pairs who need help with vocabulary or comprehension.

2. Call time and have partners answer the questions in Step 3. Remind students that they will have to teach two other students about their article.

3. Call time and have A pairs stand up and find B pairs to work with. Instruct the two sets of pairs to sit together. Review the directions for Steps 4 and 5. Check comprehension. *Do you ask questions?* [yes] *Do you read your article to the other pair?* [no]

4. Set a time limit (five minutes) for Pair B to ask Pair A questions about the A article.

5. Call time and set another time limit (five minutes) for Pair A to ask Pair B questions about the B article. Remind students that everyone in the group should be able to answer both sets of questions.

Keep Going!

Have students use the discussion prompt on the activity page to talk about a topic related to the articles.

Multilevel Suggestions

For Mixed-Level Pairs:
Pair each pre-level student with an on- or higher-level student. Have the higher-level student help the pre-level student with vocabulary and comprehension during the reading. Instruct the higher-level student to write the answers.

For Same-Level Pairs:
Pre-Level: Work with the pre-level pairs while the other groups are reading, and help them with vocabulary and comprehension as needed. Simplify the questions students ask and answer by changing them from information questions to *yes/no* questions. For example, the information question *Where does Alma live?* could be simplified to the *yes/no* question *Does Alma live in New York City?*

On-Level: Have pairs complete the project as outlined above.

Higher-Level: Provide additional questions for these students to ask each other, and have them teach each other about their articles without looking back at their papers.

Teaching Notes for the Team Project

Focus: Students work in a team to complete a project-based learning exercise.
Grouping Strategy: Teams of 3-5 students
Activity Time: 60 minutes
Student Book Connection: Review and Expand

Ready,

1. Select the Team Project activity that corresponds to the unit you're teaching in *Step Forward Student Book 3*.

2. Duplicate one copy of the activity page for each student.

3. Check the supplies and the resources needed for the project and gather enough for each team.

4. If possible, create a sample of the project students will be doing (e.g., a handbook or an advertisement).

5. Provide a review of the vocabulary and concepts students will need to complete the project.

Set...

1. Share the goal of the activity: *You're going to work in teams to create* [product]. If you have created a sample of what they'll be producing, show it to the students and answer any questions about it.

2. Have students form teams of three, four, or five. Explain the roles for the activity (see the individual activity page). Allow students to choose their jobs.

3. Ask the Supplier to pick up activity pages for his/her team.

4. As the Leaders to read the directions to their team.

5. Check comprehension by asking *yes/no* questions. *Does one person do all the work?* [no] *Do you make a list of ideas?* [yes]

6. Set a time limit (five minutes) for teams to brainstorm ideas. The Recorder writes the team's ideas while the Leader watches the clock.

Go!

1. Have students begin to create their projects. Tell students they will have 25-30 minutes to complete the project.

2. Circulate to check each team's progress.

3. About twenty minutes into the time period, check with teams to see if they need more time. Extend the time limit by five or ten minutes as needed.

4. Call "time." Have the Reporter from each team tell the class about their project.

Keep Going!

Have students complete the Keep Going activity on the Team Project activity page.

Multilevel Suggestions

For Mixed-Level Groups:
Assign pre-level students to roles that require less reading, writing, and speaking such as Supplier, Artist, and Graphic Designer. Ask higher-level students to be Leaders and Recorders.

For Same-Level Groups:
Pre-Level: Simplify the project by reducing the amount of reading and writing required. For example, with poster projects, have students label items on posters with single words.
On-Level: Have teams complete the project as outlined above.
Higher-Level: Increase the challenge for students by requiring more writing on the project. For example, have students write a paragraph on how well their team worked together.

Pre-unit The First Step

Mixers

Why Are You Learning English?

1. Think about this question: Why are you learning English?

2. Read the questions in the chart. Write 1 more question for each section.

3. Walk around the room. Find 1 classmate who answers *yes* and 1 classmate who answers *no* to each question.

Are you learning English to get a job?
Yes, I am. / No, I'm not.

4. Write your classmates' names in the correct boxes.

	Are you learning English to...	Classmates' Names	
		Yes	No
Work	get a job?		
	talk with co-workers?		
Home	help your children with their homework?		
	read the newspaper?		
Community	talk with doctors, nurses, and pharmacists?		
	talk with bank employees?		
Travel	ask for and understand directions?		
	order food and drinks?		
Culture	see American movies?		
	understand songs in English?		

KEEP GOING!

Work with a partner. Decide on the 5 most important reasons for learning English.
Put these reasons in order of importance.

What Do You Like?

1. Think about these questions: What things do you like? What things do you dislike?
2. Read the questions in the chart. Add 2 more questions.
3. Walk around the room. Find 1 classmate who likes each item and 1 classmate who dislikes it.
   Do you like pizza?
   Yes, I do. / No, I don't.
4. Write a different name in each box.

Do you like...	Classmates' Names	
	Like	Dislike
pizza?		
action movies?		
your first name?		
chocolate?		
soccer?		
winter?		
the beach?		
cats?		
coffee?		
big cities?		

KEEP GOING!
Choose 3 items in the chart. Talk to 5 classmates. Find out how many people like and dislike these items. Make a bar graph.

What Skills Do You Have?

1. Think about this question: What skills do you have?

2. Read the questions. Add 1 more question.

3. Walk around the room. Ask questions to learn about your classmates' skills.

Can you speak three languages?
Yes, I can. / No, I can't.

4. Check *yes* or *no*. Write a different name on each line.

1. Can you speak 3 languages?

☐ Yes _____
                              (name)

☐ No _____
                              (name)

2. Can you swim?

☐ Yes _____
                              (name)

☐ No _____
                              (name)

3. Can you sing a song in English?

☐ Yes _____
                              (name)

☐ No _____
                              (name)

4. Can you use a computer?

☐ Yes _____
                              (name)

☐ No _____
                              (name)

5. Can you write with your left hand?

☐ Yes _____
                              (name)

☐ No _____
                              (name)

6. Can you _____?

☐ Yes _____
                              (name)

☐ No _____
                              (name)

> **KEEP GOING!**
>
> Who can speak 3 languages? Who can write with their left hand?
> Ask these students to show the class their skills.

What Would You Like to Do?

1. Think about this question: What are some things you would like to do?

2. Read the list of questions. Add 1 more question.

3. Walk around the room. Ask questions to find out about your classmates.

Would you like to be a famous soccer player?
Yes, I would. / No, I wouldn't.

4. Check *yes* or *no*. Write a different name on each line.

1. Would you like to be a famous soccer player?

   ☐ Yes _____
                                         (name)

   ☐ No _____
                                         (name)

2. Would you like to write a book?

   ☐ Yes _____
                                         (name)

   ☐ No _____
                                         (name)

3. Would you like to travel around the world?

   ☐ Yes _____
                                         (name)

   ☐ No _____
                                         (name)

4. Would you like to be an actor on TV?

   ☐ Yes _____
                                         (name)

   ☐ No _____
                                         (name)

5. Would you like to have 20 children?

   ☐ Yes _____
                                         (name)

   ☐ No _____
                                         (name)

6. Would you like to _____?

   ☐ Yes _____
                                         (name)

   ☐ No _____
                                         (name)

KEEP GOING!

Work with a partner. Talk about other things you would like to do. Tell the class
the 2 most interesting things you and your partner would like to do.

Unit 1 Learning Together

Picture A: At the Library

1. Find a partner with Picture B (page 19).
2. Work with your partner to find 10 differences between your pictures.

3. Write the picture differences in the chart below.

	Picture A	**Picture B**
1.	*Maria is using books to do research.*	*Maria is using newspapers to do research.*
2.		
3.		
4.		
5.		
6.		
7.		
8.		
9.		
10.		

KEEP GOING!

Talk about the last time you were at a library. What did you do there?

Picture B: At the Library

1. Find a partner who has Picture A (page 18).

2. Work with your partner to find 10 differences between your pictures.

3. Write the picture differences in the chart below.

	Picture A	Picture B
1.	*Maria is using books to do research.*	*Maria is using newspapers to do research.*
2.		
3.		
4.		
5.		
6.		
7.		
8.		
9.		
10.		

KEEP GOING!

Talk about the last time you were at a library. What did you do there?

First Day of Class

1. Work with 3 classmates.
2. Look at the picture. Read the first sentence.
3. Take turns writing 1 sentence about the picture. Write as many as you can.
4. Check your spelling in a dictionary.

Yesterday was the first day of English class.

_____

_____

_____

_____

_____

_____

_____

_____

KEEP GOING!

Choose a Reporter. Have the Reporter read your 3 most interesting sentences to the class.

Study Habits

Partner A
• **Read a sentence to Partner B.** • **Listen to Partner B repeat the sentence.**   **Is it correct? If not, say it again.**
1. Every day, Carlos finds a quiet place to study. 2. Yesterday, he worked in the library. 3. He did research for his homework there. 4. Did Blanca study at the library yesterday, too?
• **Listen to Partner B say a sentence.** • **Repeat the sentence.** • **Write the sentence.**
5.
6.
7.
8.

- -FOLD HERE- -

Partner B
• **Listen to Partner A say a sentence.** • **Repeat the sentence.** • **Write the sentence.**
1.
2.
3.
4.
• **Read a sentence to Partner A.** • **Listen to Partner A repeat the sentence.**   **Is it correct? If not, say it again.**
5. Blanca didn't study at the library yesterday. 6. She always studies at home. 7. Yesterday she made an outline in her notebook. 8. Today she's memorizing new words

KEEP GOING!

Write 5 sentences about your study habits. Talk about your sentences with a partner.
I make a study schedule at the beginning of every week.

Music Then and Now

1. Read the questions. Write your answers in the chart.

2. Ask your classmates the questions in the chart.

3. Write your classmates' names and answers in the chart.

4. Use complete sentences to answer your classmates' questions.

Ask and answer these questions.	My answers	_____'s answers	_____'s answers	_____'s answers
What kind of music did you like 10 years ago?				
What kind of music do you like now?				
What kind of music will be popular in the future?				
Where did you buy music 10 years ago?				
Where do you buy music now?				
Do you usually buy music online or at a music store?				

5. Work with a partner. Compare your charts. Write 6 sentences.

Most people liked pop music 10 years ago.

1. _____
2. _____
3. _____
4. _____
5. _____
6. _____

KEEP GOING!

Was music better or worse 10 years ago? Why? Talk about your opinions with the class.

Career Choices

1. Work with 3 classmates. Say all the lines in the script.

2. Choose your character.

3. Finish the conversation. Write more lines for each character.

4. Practice the lines.

5. Act out the role-play with your group.

Scene	Characters	Props
Before class	• Student 1 • Student 2 • Student 3 • Student 4	A newspaper

The Script

Student 1: Hi. What are you doing?

Student 2: I'm looking at job ads to get some career ideas.

Student 3: What kind of career are you thinking about?

Student 2: It's hard to say.

Student 4: Well, what do you enjoy doing?

Student 2: I'm good with numbers. I also work well alone.

Student 3: Then maybe you could be an accountant.

Student 2: That's a good job. Accountants do interesting work.

Student 4: That's true. They do.

Student 1: So, what other kinds of things do you like to do?

KEEP GOING!

Watch your classmates' role-plays. Write the answers to these questions: What other careers do the students talk about? Does Student 2 decide what to do? Why or why not?

Pair A: Two Amazing Libraries

1. Find a partner with page 24. You are Pair A.

2. Read the article.

Libraries are an important part of life in the U.S. People go to libraries to do research, to use a computer, and to check out books, videos, and DVDs. There are over 117,500 libraries in the U.S., so you never have to go far to find one. And you'll be able to find any kind of library you like.

Do you like small libraries? The Coalfield Library in Coalfield, Tennessee may be the one for you. The Coalfield Library is the smallest library in the U.S. It's 5 feet long by 6 feet wide, so only two people can fit inside the library at one time! This amazing library opened in 1956 with just 75 books. It now has over 1,000 books, and they cover every inch of the library walls.

Dot Byrd was the librarian 50 years ago, and she is still the librarian today! An interviewer once asked Dot, "For how long can someone check out a book?" Dot answered, "Probably 15 or 30 years." Dot is always happy to give a "tour" of the library. She loves to show visitors around and answer questions. So if you ever visit Coalfield, be sure to stop in and see Dot. You'll be very glad you did!

3. Answer the QUESTIONS FOR PAIR A together.

QUESTIONS FOR PAIR A

   a. Where is the smallest library in the U.S.?

   _____

   b. How big is this library?

   _____

   c. Who is Dot Byrd and what does she do?

   _____

4. Find a Pair B with page 25. Answer their questions about your article.

5. Ask them the QUESTIONS TO ASK PAIR B. Write their answers.

QUESTIONS TO ASK PAIR B

   a. Where is the largest library in the U.S.?

   _____

   b. How many people visit this library each year?

   _____

   c. How can visitors learn about this library?

   _____

KEEP GOING!

Talk about these libraries. Which one would you like to visit? Why?

Pair B: Two Amazing Libraries

1. Find a partner with page 25. You are Pair B.

2. Read the article.

Libraries are an important part of life in the U.S. People go to libraries to do research, to use a computer, and to check out books, videos, and DVDs. There are over 117,500 libraries in the U.S., so you never have to go far to find one And you'll be able to find any kind of library you like.

Do you like large libraries? You can visit The Library of Congress in Washington, D.C. This amazing library opened in 1897. It is the largest library in the U.S. In fact, with more than 130 million items on 530 miles of bookshelves, it is the largest library in the world!

The Library of Congress has over 4,000 employees and more than one million visitors each year. Anyone can use the library for research, but only some government workers can check out books.

Visitors can learn about the library in two ways. They can go on a tour and see the many parts of the library with a guide. The guides are always happy to answer questions. Visitors can also watch an interesting movie about the library in the library's theater. So if you ever go to Washington, be sure to stop at the Library of Congress. You'll be very glad you did!

3. Answer the QUESTIONS FOR PAIR B together.

QUESTIONS FOR PAIR B

   a. Where is the largest library in the U.S.?

   _____

   b. How many people visit this library each year?

   _____

   c. How can visitors learn about this library?

   _____

4. Find a Pair A with page 24. Ask them the QUESTIONS TO ASK PAIR A. Write their answers.

QUESTIONS TO ASK PAIR A

   a. Where is the smallest library in the U.S.?

   _____

   b. How big is this library?

   _____

   c. Who is Dot Byrd and what does she do?

   _____

5. Answer Pair A's questions about your article.

KEEP GOING!
Talk about these libraries. Which one would you like to visit? Why?

All About Our Class

The Project: Create a handbook about your class
Supplies: construction paper, notebook paper, a stapler, colored markers and pens, or use a word processing program (if computers are available)
Resources: classroom notes, textbooks, calendars, dictionaries

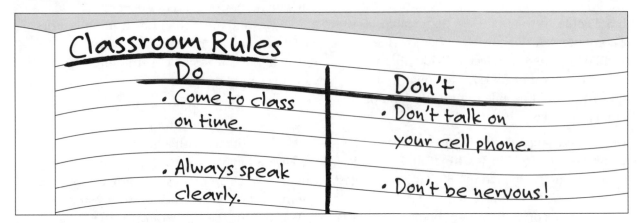

1. Work with 3–5 students. Introduce yourself.

2. Choose your job.

   Leader: Help your team work together and watch the time.
   Recorder: Write the team's ideas.
   Supplier: Get the supplies and the resources.
   Researcher: Find information to help your team complete the project.
   Reporter: Tell the class about the project.

3. As a team, choose a topic for your section of the handbook: Classroom Rules, Class Goals, Things to Bring to Class Every Day, Homework and Test Schedule, or another topic of your choice.

4. Brainstorm answers to these questions: What do you already know about your topic? What other information do you need?

   Leader: Give the team 5 minutes. Ask each person the questions.
   Recorder: Write the name and answers of each team member.
   Researcher: Find more information about your topic, and talk about it with your team.

5. Write your section.

   Supplier: Get the supplies and the resources from your teacher.
   Recorder: Write the topic of your section at the top of the paper.
   Team: Write as much information as you can about your topic. Draw pictures to help explain the information. Help the Reporter plan a class presentation.

6. Show your project to the class.

   Reporter: Tell the class about your team's section of the handbook.
   Team: Help the Reporter. Show pictures and act out some of the information.

KEEP GOING!
Put all the teams' sections together to create a class handbook.
Make a cover and a list of all the sections.

Unit 2 Ready for Some Fun

Picture A: Places to Go, Things to Do

1. Find a partner with Picture B (page 29).

2. Work with your partner to find 10 differences between your pictures.

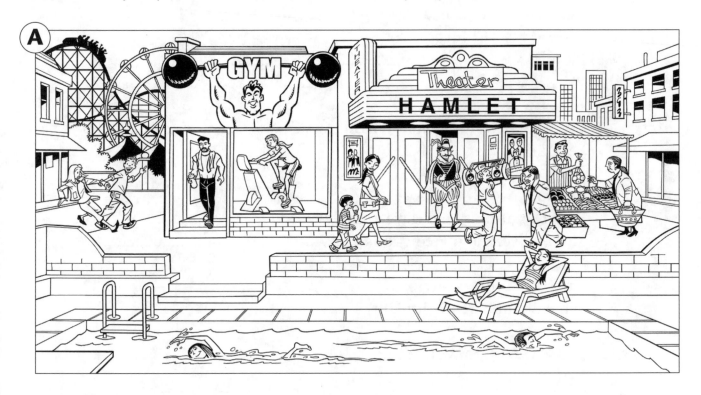

3. Write the picture differences in the chart below.

	Picture A	Picture B
1.	*The man thinks the roller coaster is exciting.*	*The man thinks the roller coaster is scary.*
2.		
3.		
4.		
5.		
6.		
7.		
8.		
9.		
10.		

KEEP GOING!
Talk about the things you do in your free time. What is your favorite recreational activity?

Picture B: Places to Go, Things to Do

1. Find a partner with Picture A (page 28).

2. Work with your partner to find 10 differences between your pictures.

3. Write the picture differences in the chart below.

	Picture A	Picture B
1.	*The man thinks the roller coaster is exciting.*	*The man thinks the roller coaster is scary.*
2.		
3.		
4.		
5.		
6.		
7.		
8.		
9.		
10.		

KEEP GOING!

Talk about the things you do in your free time. What is your favorite recreational activity?

Let's Go Out!

1. Work with 3 classmates.

2. Look at the picture. Read the first sentence.

3. Take turns writing 1 sentence about the picture. Write as many as you can.

4. Check your spelling in a dictionary.

Maria has a lot of plans for the weekend, and she wants her friend Emi to come with her.

_____

_____

_____

_____

_____

_____

_____

_____

KEEP GOING!

Choose a Reporter. Have the Reporter read your 3 most interesting sentences to the class.

We'll Have a Really Good Time

Partner A
• **Read a sentence to Partner B.** • **Listen to Partner B repeat the sentence.**   **Is it correct? If not, say it again.**
1. I'm going to have a big party on Saturday night. 2. There will be great music and a lot of food. 3. We'll have a really good time. 4. Are you going to come?
• **Listen to Partner B say a sentence.** • **Repeat the sentence.** • **Write the sentence.**
5.
6.
7.
8.

- -Fold Here- -

Partner B
• **Listen to Partner A say a sentence.** • **Repeat the sentence.** • **Write the sentence.**
1.
2.
3.
4.
• **Read a sentence to Partner A.** • **Listen to Partner A repeat the sentence.**   **Is it correct? If not, say it again.**
5. I'm going to study a little on Saturday evening. 6. I'll come to the party later. 7. I'll bring some soda, some chips, and some cheese. 8. It'll be a lot of fun!

KEEP GOING!

Write 5 sentences about your plans for next weekend. Talk about your sentences with a partner.

I'm going to see a movie with my sister next weekend.

Plans and Predictions

1. Read the questions. Write your answers in the chart.

2. Ask your classmates the questions in the chart.

3. Write your classmates' names and answers in the chart.

4. Use complete sentences to answer your classmates' questions

Ask and answer these questions.	My answers	_____'s answers	_____'s answers	_____'s answers
What are you going to do after class today?				
What are you going to have for dinner tonight?				
What is the most interesting thing you are going to do this week?				
What is the most important thing you are going to do this year?				
What do you think you will learn this year?				
Where do you think you will live in 5 years?				

5. Work with a partner. Compare your charts. Write 6 sentences.

Some people are going to go shopping after class, but most people are going to go home.

1. _____

2. _____

3. _____

4. _____

5. _____

6. _____

KEEP GOING!

Who has the most interesting plans? Talk about your opinions with the class.

What Should We Do Tonight?

1. Work with 3 classmates. Say all the lines in the script.

2. Choose your character.

3. Finish the conversation. Write more lines for each character.

4. Practice the lines.

5. Act out the role-play with your group.

Scene	Characters	Props
An apartment	• Jan • Pat • Lee • Sam	A newspaper

The Script

Jan: We should go out and do something tonight.

Pat: Good idea. What would you like to do?

Jan: Well, we could see a movie. Should I check the movie schedule?

Lee: No, thanks. I went to the movies yesterday.

Pat: I think I'd rather go to the mall.

Lee: But I don't need to go shopping.

Sam: We could go dancing.

Lee: No. I'm a terrible dancer.

Sam: Well, what do you want to do?

Lee: It's up to you.

KEEP GOING!

Watch your classmates' role-plays. Write the answers to these questions: What other ideas do the friends have? What do they finally decide to do?

Pair A: Extreme Sports

1. Find a partner with page 34. You are Pair A.

2. Read the article.

Everyone has a favorite recreational activity. Some people like to walk or run. Others like to play sports such as soccer or football. But some people want more exciting activities. These people play extreme sports. Extreme sports are scarier and more dangerous than the sports most people enjoy. Extreme sports are full of danger, action, and excitement.

One popular extreme sport is buildering. Builderers climb up the outside of buildings. They usually do not use safety equipment. They use only their hands and special climbing shoes. This is very difficult and dangerous.

One of the most famous builderers is Alain Robert, from France. How did Alain begin? One day when he was 12 years old, Alain forgot his keys. He was locked out of his eighth-floor apartment. So he climbed up the outside wall of the apartment building to get in!

Since that time, Alain has climbed the Eiffel Tower in France, the Empire State Building in New York, and the Petronas Towers in Kuala Lumpur, Malaysia. Buildering taught Alain an important lesson, and he likes to share it with others. He says that we are all strong enough to set high goals and to do the things we want to do.

3. Answer the QUESTIONS FOR PAIR A together.

QUESTIONS FOR PAIR A

   a. What do builderers do?

   _____

   b. What was the first building Alain Robert climbed? Why?

   _____

   c. What other buildings did he climb?

   _____

4. Find a Pair B with page 35. Answer their questions about your article.

5. Ask them the QUESTIONS TO ASK PAIR B. Write their answers.

QUESTIONS TO ASK PAIR B

   a. What is free diving?

   _____

   b. Why is Tanya Streeter the world's best free diver?

   _____

   c. How did Tanya's love of water begin?

   _____

KEEP GOING!
Talk about extreme sports. Would you like to try an extreme sport? Why or why not?

Pair B: Extreme Sports

1. Find a partner with page 35. You are Pair B.

2. Read the article.

Everyone has a favorite recreational activity. Some people like to walk or run. Others like to play sports such as soccer or football. But some people want more exciting activities. These people play extreme sports. Extreme sports are scarier and more dangerous than the sports most of us enjoy. Extreme sports are full of danger, action, and excitement.

One popular extreme sport is free diving. Free divers take one deep breath of air, and then they go hundreds of feet under water. They try to stay down as long as they can. The divers don't use any safety equipment, so this is a very difficult and dangerous sport.

Tanya Streeter is the world's best free diver. In 2003, she stayed under 400 feet of water for 3 minutes and 38 seconds. Tanya began to love the water when she was a child in the Cayman Islands. She spent all of her days in the ocean just like a fish! You might think Tanya is not afraid of anything, but that's not true. She says that she is afraid of the dark. And she doesn't like heights or roller coasters. But the water is a different story. Under water, Tanya feels completely at home.

3. Answer the QUESTIONS FOR PAIR B together.

QUESTIONS FOR PAIR B

　a. What is free diving?

　_____

　b. Why is Tanya Streeter the world's best free diver?

　_____

　c. How did Tanya's love of the water begin?

　_____

4. Find a Pair A with page 34. Ask them the QUESTIONS TO ASK PAIR A. Write their answers.

QUESTIONS TO ASK PAIR A

　a. What do builderers do?

　_____

　b. What was the first building Alain Robert climbed? Why?

　_____

　c. What other buildings did Alain climb?

　_____

5. Answer Pair A's questions about your article.

KEEP GOING!
Talk about extreme sports. Would you like to try an extreme sport? Why or why not?

On the Go!

The Project: Create a poster about a recreational activity
Supplies: poster board, markers or colored pencils, magazines, scissors, glue
Resources: magazines on sports, arts and crafts, gardening, and other recreational activities, or information about these activities on the Internet, dictionaries

1. Work with 3–5 students. Introduce yourself.

2. Choose your job.

   Leader: Help your team work together and watch the time.
   Recorder: Write the team's ideas.
   Supplier: Get the supplies and the resources.
   Researcher: Find information to help your team complete the project.
   Reporter: Tell the class about the project.

3. As a team, choose a recreational activity for your poster: soccer, tennis, walking, dancing, gardening, or another activity of your choice.

4. Brainstorm answers to these questions: What do you already know about your activity? Do you need special equipment and clothing? Are there rules? What are some helpful tips?

   Leader: Give the team 10 minutes. Ask each person the questions.
   Recorder: Write the name and answers of each team member.
   Researcher: Find more information about the activity, and talk about it with your team.

5. Create the poster.

   Supplier: Get the supplies and the resources from your teacher.
   Recorder: Write the name of the activity at the top of the poster.
   Team: Organize the information into groups (equipment, rules, tips). Write as much information as you can. Add photos or drawings. Help the Reporter plan a class presentation.

6. Show your project to the class.

   Reporter: Tell the class about your team's poster.
   Team: Point to the parts of the poster as the Reporter explains them.

> **KEEP GOING!**
> After the teams present their posters, choose one activity you would like to try.
> Talk about the reasons for your choice.

Unit 3 A Job to Do

Picture A: Computers at Work

1. Find a partner with Picture B (page 39).

2. Work with your partner to find 10 differences between your pictures.

3. Write the picture differences in the chart below.

	Picture A	Picture B
1.	*Tara's computer doesn't show her desktop.*	*Tara's computer shows her desktop.*
2.		
3.		
4.		
5.		
6.		
7.		
8.		
9.		
10.		

KEEP GOING!

Talk about different jobs that use computers. Would you like to have
any of these jobs? Why or why not?

Picture B: Computers at Work

1. Find a partner with Picture A (page 38).

2. Work with your partner to find 10 differences between your pictures.

3. Write the picture differences in the chart below.

	Picture A	Picture B
1.	*Tara's computer doesn't show her desktop.*	*Tara's computer shows her desktop.*
2.		
3.		
4.		
5.		
6.		
7.		
8.		
9.		
10.		

KEEP GOING!

Talk about different jobs that use computers. Would you like to have any of these jobs? Why or why not?

An Awful Office

1. Work with 3 classmates.

2. Look at the picture. Read the first sentence.

3. Take turns writing 1 sentence about the picture. Write as many as you can.

4. Check your spelling in a dictionary.

There are a lot of problems in the Apex Company office.

_____

_____

_____

_____

_____

_____

_____

_____

KEEP GOING!

Choose a Reporter. Have the Reporter read your 3 most interesting sentences to the class.

Comparing Jobs

Partner A
• **Read a sentence to Partner B.** • **Listen to Partner B repeat the sentence.**   **Is it correct? If not, say it again.**
1. Tim's new job is less stressful than his old job. 2. The people are friendlier. 3. The office is not as far from home as his old office. 4. His new job is as interesting as his old job.
• **Listen to Partner B say a sentence.** • **Repeat the sentence.** • **Write the sentence.**
5.
6.
7.
8.

- -FOLD HERE- -

Partner B
• **Listen to Partner A say a sentence.** • **Repeat the sentence.** • **Write the sentence.**
1.
2.
3.
4.
• **Read a sentence to Partner A.** • **Listen to Partner B repeat the sentence.**   **Is it correct? If not, say it again.**
5. Some things are more difficult at Tim's new job. 6. His manager is not as helpful as his old manager. 7. He has the smallest office and the least powerful computer. 8. He has to work more hours than he worked at his old job.

> **KEEP GOING!**
> Write 5 sentences that compare people, places, or things at your school or work.
> Talk about your sentences with a partner.
> *My dictionary is not as heavy as my textbook.*

Shopping Around Town

1. Read the questions in the chart. Write your answers in the chart.

2. Ask your classmates the questions in the chart.

3. Write your classmates' names and answers in the chart.

4. Use complete sentences to answer your classmates' questions.

Do you think . . .	My answers	_____'s answers	_____'s answers	_____'s answers
clothing stores are as interesting as computer stores?				
supermarkets are as expensive as farmers markets?				
music stores are more popular than book stores?				
home improvement stores are more fun than shoe stores?				
salespeople in large stores are less friendly than salespeople in small stores?				

5. Work with a partner. Compare your charts. Write 6 sentences.

I think clothing stores are as interesting as computer stores, but Jane thinks computer stores are more interesting.

1. _____

2. _____

3. _____

4. _____

5. _____

6. _____

KEEP GOING!
What are the best places in your town to buy clothes, music, and food?

A Talk After Class

1. Work with 2 classmates. Say all the lines in the script.

2. Choose your character.

3. Finish the conversation. Write more lines for each character.

4. Practice the lines.

5. Act out the role-play with your group.

Scene	Characters	Props
After class	• Teacher • Student 1 • Student 2	Three chairs

The Script

Teacher: Can you both stay for a minute, please?

Student 1: Of course.

Student 2: Sure.

Teacher: Please sit down. You know, you two are the most creative students in my class.

Student 2: Thanks!

Teacher: But you need to pay attention.

Student 1: I'm sorry.

Student 2: Thanks for letting us know.

Student 1: You won't have to tell us again.

Teacher: Good. And there's one more thing.

KEEP GOING!

Watch your classmates' role-plays. Write the answers to these questions: What other problems does the teacher talk about? What do the students say to the teacher?

Pair A: Learning on the Job

1. Find a partner with page 44. You are Pair A.

2. Read the email.

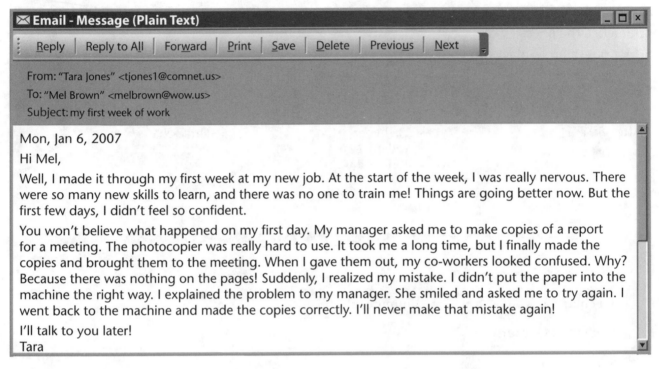

3. Answer the QUESTIONS FOR PAIR A together.

QUESTIONS FOR PAIR A

   a. What did Tara's manager ask her to do on her first day of work?

   _____

   b. What was the problem with the copies?

   _____

   c. What mistake did Tara make?

   _____

4. Find a Pair B with page 45. Answer their questions about your article.

5. Ask them the QUESTIONS TO ASK PAIR B. Write their answers.

QUESTIONS TO ASK PAIR B

   a. What did Tara's manager ask her to do on her second day of work?

   _____

   b. Who did she write an email to?

   _____

   c. What mistake did she make?

   _____

> **KEEP GOING!**
>
> Talk about learning to use technology. Do most managers act like Tara's manager?

Pair B: Learning on the Job

1. Find a partner with page 45. You are Pair B.

2. Read the email.

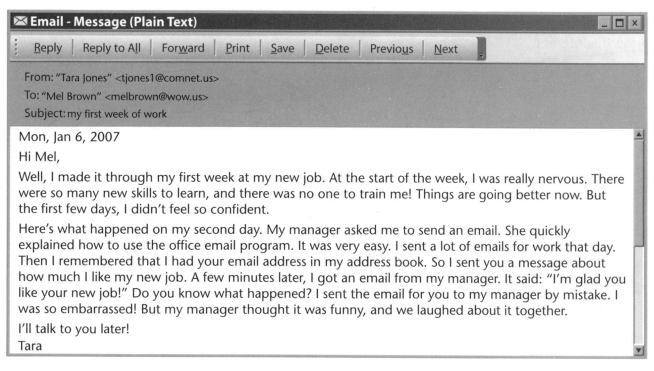

✉ **Email - Message (Plain Text)**   _ □ ✕

⋮   <u>R</u>eply | Reply to A<u>l</u>l | For<u>w</u>ard | <u>P</u>rint | <u>S</u>ave | <u>D</u>elete | Previo<u>u</u>s | <u>N</u>ext

From: "Tara Jones" <tjones1@comnet.us>
To: "Mel Brown" <melbrown@wow.us>
Subject: my first week of work

Mon, Jan 6, 2007

Hi Mel,

Well, I made it through my first week at my new job. At the start of the week, I was really nervous. There were so many new skills to learn, and there was no one to train me! Things are going better now. But the first few days, I didn't feel so confident.

Here's what happened on my second day. My manager asked me to send an email. She quickly explained how to use the office email program. It was very easy. I sent a lot of emails for work that day. Then I remembered that I had your email address in my address book. So I sent you a message about how much I like my new job. A few minutes later, I got an email from my manager. It said: "I'm glad you like your new job!" Do you know what happened? I sent the email for you to my manager by mistake. I was so embarrassed! But my manager thought it was funny, and we laughed about it together.

I'll talk to you later!
Tara

3. Answer the QUESTIONS FOR PAIR B together.

QUESTIONS FOR PAIR B

   a. What did Tara's manager ask her to do on her second day of work?

   _____

   b. Who did she write an email to?

   _____

   c. What mistake did she make?

   _____

4. Find a Pair A with page 44. Ask them the QUESTIONS TO ASK PAIR A. Write their answers.

QUESTIONS TO ASK PAIR A

   a. What did Tara's manager ask her to do on her first day of work?

   _____

   b. What was the problem with the copies?

   _____

   c. What mistake did Tara make?

   _____

5. Answer Pair A's questions about your article.

> **KEEP GOING!**
> Talk about learning to use technology. Do most managers act like Tara's manager?

What Our Classroom Needs

The Project: Choose a new piece of equipment for your classroom
Supplies: notebook paper, letter paper, an envelope, and pens, or use a word processing program (if computers are available)
Resources: dictionaries, newspapers, magazines, office equipment catalogs as brochures or on the Internet

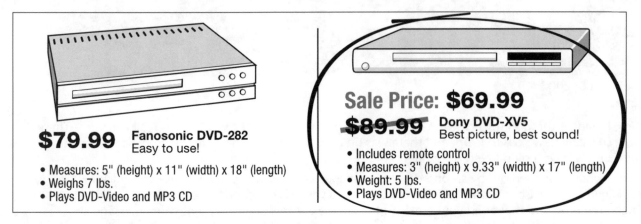

$79.99 **Fanosonic DVD-282**
Easy to use!

- Measures: 5" (height) x 11" (width) x 18" (length)
- Weighs 7 lbs.
- Plays DVD-Video and MP3 CD

Sale Price: $69.99
~~$89.99~~ **Dony DVD-XV5**
Best picture, best sound!

- Includes remote control
- Measures: 3" (height) x 9.33" (width) x 17" (length)
- Weight: 5 lbs.
- Plays DVD-Video and MP3 CD

1. Work with 3–5 students. Introduce yourself.

2. Choose your job.

> **Leader:** Help your team work together and watch the time.
> **Recorder:** Write the team's ideas.
> **Supplier:** Get the supplies and the resources.
> **Researcher:** Find information to help your team complete the project.
> **Reporter:** Tell the class about the project.

3. Brainstorm answers to these questions: What equipment does your classroom need most? What information do you need before you buy this item?

> **Leader:** Give the team 5 minutes. Ask each person the questions.
> **Recorder:** Write the name and answers of each team member.

4. As a team, choose a piece of equipment and research it.

> **Supplier:** Get the supplies and the resources from your teacher.
> **Team:**
> - Choose a piece of equipment for your classroom.
> - Find ads for this equipment.
> - Compare the information in the ads. Decide on the best product for your class.
> **Researcher:** Use a dictionary to help your team with vocabulary.

5. Tell the class about your project.

> **Reporter:** Tell the class about the product your team chose. Explain your reasons.

KEEP GOING!

With your classmates, decide which team's product is best. Write a letter to your school administrator to request this product for your class.

Unit 4 Good Work

Picture A: Will She Get the Job?

1. Find a partner with Picture B (page 49).

2. Work with your partner to find 10 differences between your pictures.

3. Write the picture differences in the chart below.

	Picture A	**Picture B**
1.	*Alison is dressed professionally.*	*Alison is dressed inappropriately.*
2.		
3.		
4.		
5.		
6.		
7.		
8.		
9.		
10.		

KEEP GOING!

Talk about job interviews. Did you ever have one? If so, talk about your experience.

Picture B: Will She Get the Job?

1. Find a partner with Picture A (page 48).

2. Work with your partner to find 10 differences between your pictures.

Mrs. Garcia   Alison

3. Write the picture differences in the chart below.

	Picture A	**Picture B**
1.	*Alison is dressed professionally.*	*Alison is dressed inappropriately.*
2.		
3.		
4.		
5.		
6.		
7.		
8.		
9.		
10.		

KEEP GOING!

Talk about job interviews. Did you ever have one? If so, talk about your experience.

Tell Me About Yourself

1. Work with 3 classmates.
2. Look at the picture. Read the first sentence.
3. Take turns writing 1 sentence about the picture. Write as many as you can.
4. Check your spelling in a dictionary.

George thinks he has the right skills and experience for this job.

KEEP GOING!
Choose a Reporter. Have the Reporter read your 3 most interesting sentences to the class.

The Right Person for the Job

Partner A
• **Read a sentence to Partner B.** • **Listen to Partner B repeat the sentence.**   **Is it correct? If not, say it again.**
1. We have needed a new receptionist for a long time. 2. We have looked at many resumes. 3. We have interviewed a lot of people. 4. We haven't found the right person for the job.
• **Listen to Partner B say a sentence.** • **Repeat the sentence.** • **Write the sentence.**
5.
6.
7.
8.

- Fold Here -

Partner B
• **Listen to Partner A say a sentence.** • **Repeat the sentence.** • **Write the sentence.**
1.
2.
3.
4.
• **Read a sentence to Partner A.** • **Listen to Partner A repeat the sentence.**   **Is it correct? If not, say it again.**
5. I think I have found a great person for the job. 6. She has worked as a receptionist for more than ten years. 7. She has had a lot of experience in different kinds of offices. 8. I have asked her to come in for an interview.

KEEP GOING!

Write 5 sentences about things you have done in the last 10 years. Talk about your sentences with a partner.
I have worked in a supermarket.

Work Experiences

1. Read the questions. Write your answers in the chart.

2. Ask your classmates the questions in the chart.

3. Write your classmates' names and answers in the chart.

4. Use complete sentences to answer your classmates' questions.

In the last 5 years, have you . . .	My answers	_____'s answers	_____'s answers	_____'s answers
had an office job?				
had an outdoor job?				
had a job that you enjoyed?				
had a boring job?				
had a good manager?				
had a terrible manager?				

5. Work with a partner. Compare your charts. Write 6 sentences.

Most people have not had an office job in the last 5 years.

1. _____

2. _____

3. _____

4. _____

5. _____

6. _____

KEEP GOING!

What makes a job good? Describe the perfect job. Talk about your opinions with the class.

Pair B: Speaking Without Words

1. Find a partner with page 55. You are Pair B.

2. Read the article.

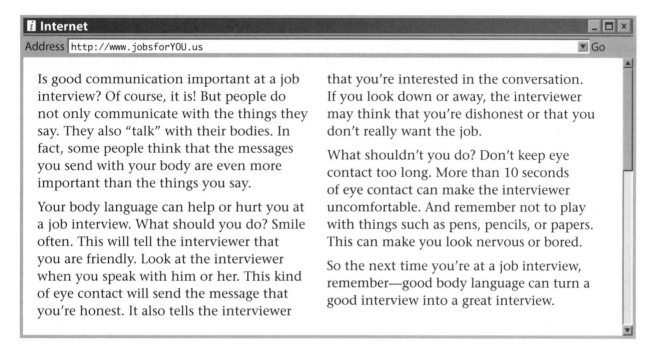

Internet

Address `http://www.jobsforYOU.us` ▼ Go

Is good communication important at a job interview? Of course, it is! But people do not only communicate with the things they say. They also "talk" with their bodies. In fact, some people think that the messages you send with your body are even more important than the things you say.

Your body language can help or hurt you at a job interview. What should you do? Smile often. This will tell the interviewer that you are friendly. Look at the interviewer when you speak with him or her. This kind of eye contact will send the message that you're honest. It also tells the interviewer

that you're interested in the conversation. If you look down or away, the interviewer may think that you're dishonest or that you don't really want the job.

What shouldn't you do? Don't keep eye contact too long. More than 10 seconds of eye contact can make the interviewer uncomfortable. And remember not to play with things such as pens, pencils, or papers. This can make you look nervous or bored.

So the next time you're at a job interview, remember—good body language can turn a good interview into a great interview.

3. Answer the QUESTIONS FOR PAIR B together.

QUESTIONS FOR PAIR B

   a. What are two examples of body language that can help you at an interview?

   _____

   b. What are two examples of body language that may hurt you at an interview?

   _____

   c. Why shouldn't you play with things such as pencils, pens, or papers?

   _____

4. Find a Pair A with page 54. Ask them the QUESTIONS TO ASK PAIR A. Write their answers.

QUESTIONS TO ASK PAIR A

   a. Why are handshakes important at a job interview?

   _____

   b. What message does a strong handshake send?

   _____

   c. Describe two unsuccessful handshakes.

   _____

5. Answer Pair A's questions about your article.

> **KEEP GOING!**
> What advice in these readings might be the hardest for you to follow at an interview? Why?

What Makes You a Great Employee?

The Project: Create a survey about work skills and personal strengths
Supplies: notebook paper and pens, or use a word processing program (if computers are available)
Resources: dictionaries

Job Skills Survey		
1. I can use a computer.	Yes	No
2. I can type quickly.	Yes	No
3. I am a team player.	Yes	No
4.		
5.		
6.		

1. Work with 3–5 students. Introduce yourself.

2. Choose your job.

> **Leader:** Help your team work together and watch the time.
> **Recorder:** Write the team's ideas.
> **Supplier:** Get the supplies and the resources.
> **Researcher:** Find information to help your team complete the project.
> **Reporter:** Tell the class about the project.

3. Brainstorm answers to this question: What are some skills and personal strengths that are important on the job?

> **Leader:** Give the team 5 minutes. Ask each person the question.
> **Recorder:** Write the name and answers of each team member.

4. Create the survey.

> **Supplier:** Get the supplies and the resources from your teacher.
> **Team:**
> • Write a list of 8–10 sentences about work skills and personal strengths.
> • Number the sentences and write *Yes* and *No* next to each one.
> • If possible, make copies of your survey for your classmates.
> **Researcher:** Use a dictionary to help your team with vocabulary and spelling.

5. Show your project to the class.

> **Reporter:** Ask another team to complete your team's survey. Read them the questions or give them a copy.

KEEP GOING!
After another team has completed your survey, look at their answers.
Talk about the results with your team.

Unit 5 Community Resources

Picture A: Can You Pick Me Up?

1. Find a partner who has Picture B (page 59).

2. Work with your partner to find 10 differences between your pictures.

3. Write the picture differences in the chart below.

	Picture A	**Picture B**
1.	*Charlie is at the clinic because he's sick.*	*Charlie is at the clinic for a wellness checkup.*
2.		
3.		
4.		
5.		
6.		
7.		
8.		
9.		
10.		

KEEP GOING!

Talk about your community. What is your favorite place to visit? What do you do there?

Picture B: Can You Pick Me Up?

1. Find a partner with Picture A (page 58).

2. Work with your partner to find 10 differences between your pictures.

3. Write the picture differences in the chart below.

	Picture A	Picture B
1.	*Charlie is at the clinic because he's sick.*	*Charlie is at the clinic for a wellness checkup.*
2.		
3.		
4.		
5.		
6.		
7.		
8.		
9.		
10.		

KEEP GOING!

Talk about your community. What is your favorite place to visit? What do you do there?

Problems in the Park

1. Work with 3 classmates.

2. Look at the picture. Read the first sentence.

3. Take turns writing 1 sentence about the picture. Write as many as you can.

4. Check your spelling in a dictionary.

Teresa is angry about all of the problems in Johnson Park.

_____

_____

_____

_____

_____

_____

_____

_____

KEEP GOING!

Choose a Reporter. Have the Reporter read your 3 most interesting sentences to the class.

Animal Adoption

Partner A
• **Read a sentence to Partner B.** • **Listen to Partner B repeat the sentence.**   **Is it correct? If not, say it again.**
1. Has Rosa gone to the animal shelter yet? 2. Yes, she has already been there. 3. Has she chosen a pet yet? 4. Yes, she has adopted two big cats.
• **Listen to Partner B say a sentence.** • **Repeat the sentence.** • **Write the sentence.**
5.
6.
7.
8.

- Fold Here -

Partner B
• **Listen to Partner A say a sentence.** • **Repeat the sentence.** • **Write the sentence.**
1.
2.
3.
4.
• **Read a sentence to Partner A.** • **Listen to Partner A repeat the sentence.**   **Is it correct? If not, say it again.**
5. Has Rosa given the cats names yet? 6. Yes, she has already named them Pam and Sam. 7. Has she told her husband about the cats? 8. No, she hasn't said anything about them yet.

KEEP GOING!

Write 5 questions about experiences at places in the community. Give your list of
questions to your partner. Ask your partner to write answers.
Have you gone swimming at the recreation center yet? / Yes, I have.

Things You Have Done

1. Read the questions. Write your answers in the chart.
2. Ask your classmates the questions in the chart.
3. Write your classmates' names and answers in the chart.
4. Use complete sentences to answer your classmates' questions.

Have you ever . . .?	My answers	_____'s answers	_____'s answers	_____'s answers
bought something online?				
been to a farmers market?				
used a digital camera?				
gone on a job interview?				
been on a roller coaster?				
adopted a pet?				

5. Work with a partner. Compare your charts. Write 6 sentences.

Marta and I have bought things online, but Diego and Reiko haven't.

1. _____
2. _____
3. _____
4. _____
5. _____
6. _____

KEEP GOING!

What are the most interesting experiences you have had in your life so far?
Describe them to the class.

Community Petition

1. Work with 2 classmates. Say all the lines in the script.
2. Choose your character.
3. Finish the conversation. Write more lines for each character.
4. Practice the lines.
5. Act out the role-play with your group.

Scene	Characters	Props
At the front door of a home	• Neighbor 1 • Neighbor 2 • Neighbor 3	• A clipboard with a piece of paper • A pen

The Script

Neighbor 1: Hello. We're from the Chester Community Action Group.

Neighbor 2: Did you get the letter we sent about our petition?

Neighbor 3: Yes, I did. But I'm sorry. I haven't read it yet.

Neighbor 1: That's OK. Do you have a minute so we can tell you about it?

Neighbor 3: Sure.

Neighbor 2: We want the town to put streetlights on this street.

Neighbor 3: Is that really necessary?

Neighbor 2: Oh, yes. This street is very dangerous at night. The drivers can't see the pedestrians

Neighbor 1: There have been several accidents over the last few years.

Neighbor 3: Yes, I know. But I'm not sure streetlights are a good idea.

KEEP GOING!

Watch your classmates' role-plays. Write the answers to these questions: What is Neighbor 3 worried about? Does Neighbor 3 decide to sign the petition?

Pair A: Small Towns, Funny Names

1. Find a partner with page 64. You are Pair A.

2. Read the article.

What do *Telephone, Left Hand, and Eighty Four*[1] have in common? They are all names of small towns in the U.S.! In fact, there are hundreds of U.S. towns that have funny names. And there are many interesting stories about how the towns got their names.

Some American towns are named after foods or even drinks! For example, there's Hot Coffee, Mississippi. Hot Coffee got its name in the early 1800s. There was a small hotel that sold hot coffee to travelers. The hotel put up a sign that said, "Hot Coffee." People who passed the building often said, "Let's go to Hot Coffee," so that became the name of the hotel. Soon, Hot Coffee became the name of the whole town.

Another example is Tea, South Dakota. In 1902 the citizens had a meeting to choose a town name. The meeting went on for a long time, but no one had any ideas. After a while, they took a break to have some tea. During the break, someone suggested *Tea* as a possible name. Everyone liked that idea, so that's what they named the town!

Do you know any funny town names? Try to find one on a map. Do some research to learn how the town got its name. You might find a surprising story!

[1]Telephone, Texas; Left Hand, West Virginia; Eighty Four, Pennsylvania

3. Answer the QUESTIONS FOR PAIR A together.

QUESTIONS FOR PAIR A

  a. What are some American towns named after?

  _____

  b. How did Hot Coffee, Mississippi get its name?

  _____

  c. How did Tea, South Dakota get its name?

  _____

4. Find a Pair B with page 65. Answer their questions about your article.

5. Ask them the QUESTIONS TO ASK PAIR B. Write their answers.

QUESTIONS TO ASK PAIR B

  a. What are some American towns with positive names?

  _____

  b. How did Boring, Oregon get its name?

  _____

  c. How did Uncertain, Texas get its name?

  _____

KEEP GOING!
Imagine your town has no name. Decide on a good name for your town.

Pair B: Small Towns, Funny Names

1. Find a partner with page 65. You are Pair B.

2. Read the article.

What do *Telephone, Left Hand,* and *Eighty Four*[1] have in common? They are all names of small towns in the U.S.! In fact, there are hundreds of U.S. towns that have funny names. And there are many interesting stories about how the towns got their names.

Some American town names sound positive For example, there's Happy, Texas; Success, Missouri; and Celebration Florida Other towns like Boring, Oregon; Uncertain, Texas; and Why, Arizona sound less positive. Citizens of Boring laugh about their Boring stores, Boring restaurants, and Boring schools. How did the town get its name? The story is actually a little… well…boring. The town is named for W. H. Boring, an old man who lived there once.

The story of Uncertain's name is more interesting. From 1836 to 1845, Texas was its own country, the Republic of Texas. People in Texas were uncertain—they weren't sure—if they were citizens of the U.S. or citizens of the Republic. So one group of Texans named their town Uncertain. Why is also a town name that sounds uncertain. But there's a town in North Carolina with a name that gives a certain answer: Whynot.

Do you know any funny town names? Try to find one on a map. Do some research to learn how the town got its name. You might find a surprising story!

[1]Telephone, Texas; Left Hand, West Virginia; Eighty Four, Pennsylvania

3. Answer the QUESTIONS FOR PAIR B together.

QUESTIONS FOR PAIR B

   a. What are some American towns that have positive names?

   _____

   b. How did Boring, Oregon get its name?

   _____

   c. How did Uncertain, Texas get its name?

   _____

4. Find a Pair A with page 64. Ask them the QUESTIONS TO ASK PAIR A. Write their answers.

QUESTIONS TO ASK PAIR A

   a. What are some American towns named after?

   _____

   b. How did Hot Coffee, Mississippi get its name?

   _____

   c. How did Tea, South Dakota get its name?

   _____

5. Answer Pair A's questions about your article.

> **KEEP GOING!**
> Imagine your town has no name. Decide on a good name for your town.

The Best Places in Town

The Project: Create a class community guide
Supplies: construction paper, notebook paper, a stapler, pens, or use a word processing program (if computers are available)
Resources: dictionaries, yellow pages, or community information in brochures or on the Internet

Restaurants in Our Town

○	Name	Address	Phone	Description
	Bay Pizza	167 Common Avenue	(978) 555-6756	informal, inexpensive
	Kathy's Cafe'	122 Brown Street	(978) 555-9834	best burgers in town, inexpensive
	The Lotus	321 Main Street	(978) 555-1343	take-out Chinese food, inexpensive
	Luigi's Italian Restaurant	45 Main Street	(978) 555-1450	romantic, very expensive
	Siam Village	231 Common Avenue	(978) 555-3787	great Thai food, inexpensive

1. Work with 3–5 students. Introduce yourself.

2. Choose your job.

Leader: Help your team work together and watch the time.
Recorder: Write the team's ideas.
Supplier: Get the supplies and the resources.
Researcher: Find information to help your team complete the project.
Reporter: Tell the class about the project.

3. As a team, choose a section of the guide to research: Community Services, Restaurants, Entertainment, Stores, or another section of your choice.

4. Brainstorm some places to list in your section of the guide. Describe them.

Leader: Give the team 10 minutes. Ask each person to name and describe places.
Recorder: Write the name and ideas of each team member.
Researcher: Find more information about places, and talk about it with your team.

5. Write your section of the guide.

Supplier: Get the supplies and resources from your teacher.
Recorder: Write the title of your section at the top of the page.
Team:
 • List the names of places for your section.
 • Add addresses, phone numbers, and descriptions.
 • Help the Reporter plan a class presentation.

6. Show your project to the class.

Reporter: Tell the class about the 3 most interesting places in your team's section of the guide.

KEEP GOING!

Put all the teams' sections together to create a class community guide. Make a cover and a list of the sections. Keep the guide in the classroom library for new students' future use.

Unit 6 What's Cooking?

Picture A: In the Kitchen

1. Find a partner with Picture B (page 69).

2. Work with your partner to find 10 differences between your pictures.

3. Write the picture differences in the chart below.

	Picture A	Picture B
1.	*The woman is cutting a potato.*	*The woman is peeling a potato.*
2.		
3.		
4.		
5.		
6.		
7.		
8.		
9.		
10.		

KEEP GOING!

Talk about kitchen items. In your opinion, what are the five most important ones?
How many uses can you think of for each item?

Picture B: In the Kitchen

1. Find a partner with Picture A (page 68).

2. Work with your partner to find 10 differences between your pictures.

3. Write the picture differences in the chart below.

	Picture A	**Picture B**
1.	*The woman is cutting a potato.*	*The woman is peeling a potato.*
2.		
3.		
4.		
5.		
6.		
7.		
8.		
9.		
10.		

KEEP GOING!

Talk about kitchen items. In your opinion, what are the five most important ones?
How many uses can you think of for each item?

A Home-cooked Dinner

1. Work with 3 classmates.
2. Look at the picture. Read the first sentence.
3. Take turns writing 1 sentence about the picture. Write as many as you can.
4. Check your spelling in a dictionary.

When Mariko was a child, her favorite dish was yakisoba.

_____

_____

_____

_____

_____

_____

_____

_____

KEEP GOING!
Choose a Reporter. Have the Reporter read your 3 most interesting sentences to the class.

Clean Up Quickly!

Partner A
• **Read a sentence to Partner B.** • **Listen to Partner B repeat the sentence.**   **Is it correct? If not, say it again.**
1. Please clean up the living room quickly. 2. My friends are coming over very soon. 3. Take the vacuum cleaner out of the closet and turn it on. 4. Please vacuum the rug as fast as you can.
• **Listen to Partner B say a sentence.** • **Repeat the sentence.** • **Write the sentence.**
5.
6.
7.
8.

- FOLD HERE -

Partner B
• **Listen to Partner A say a sentence.** • **Repeat the sentence.** • **Write the sentence.**
1.
2.
3.
4.
• **Read a sentence to Partner A.** • **Listen to Partner A repeat the sentence.**   **Is it correct? If not, say it again.**
5. Please turn off the vacuum cleaner for a minute. 6. You need to put in a new vacuum cleaner bag. 7. Look for the new bags in the kitchen closet. 8. Don't forget to take out the garbage, too.

KEEP GOING!

Write 5 sentences about things you do in your home. Talk about your sentences with a partner.
I turn off the lights at night.

In Your Opinion

1. Read the questions. Write your answers in the chart.

2. Ask your classmates the questions in the chart.

3. Write your classmates' names and answers in the chart.

4. Use complete sentences to answer your classmates' questions.

Ask and answer these questions.	My answers	_____'s answers	_____'s answers	_____'s answers
Is it more important to cut down on sugar or salt?				
Is it more difficult to look after a baby or a 5 year old child?				
Is it harder to figure out a bar graph or a pie chart?				
Is it more fun to shop for other people or for yourself?				
Is it more relaxing to pick up a book or turn on the TV?				

5. Work with a partner. Compare your charts. Write 6 sentences.

Most people think it is more important to cut down on salt than on sugar.

1. _____

2. _____

3. _____

4. _____

5. _____

6. _____

KEEP GOING!

Do most students have the same opinion or a different opinion about each question? Explain your answer with examples.

That's Not What I Ordered

1. Work with 2 classmates. Say all the lines in the script.
2. Choose your character.
3. Finish the conversation. Write more lines for each character.
4. Practice the lines.
5. Act out the role-play with your group.

Scene	Characters	Props
A restaurant	• Server • Friend 1 • Friend 2	• Two chairs • A table

The Script

Server: How is your chicken?

Friend 1: Well, it's OK, but it's not very spicy.

Friend 2: Mine is very spicy. I think I'll have to order something else.

Server: Oh, I'm sorry. What else can I get for you?

Friend 1: Wait a minute. I love spicy food. Could I try some of yours?

Friend 2: Sure. Take this piece.

Friend 1: Mmm. That's great. Do you want to try mine?

Friend 2: Thanks. Mmmmm. Delicious. It tastes like sweet and sour chicken.

Server: Oh, I'm so sorry. I know what happened.

KEEP GOING!

Watch your classmates' role-plays. Write the answers to these questions: What does the server say next? What do the friends say to the server?

Pair A: Fad Diets

1. Find a partner with page 74. You are Pair A.

2. Read the article.

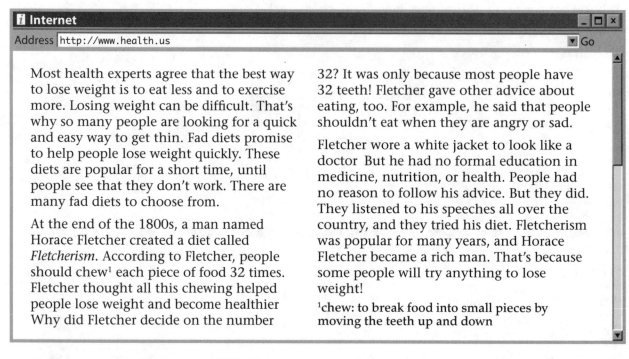

Most health experts agree that the best way to lose weight is to eat less and to exercise more. Losing weight can be difficult. That's why so many people are looking for a quick and easy way to get thin. Fad diets promise to help people lose weight quickly. These diets are popular for a short time, until people see that they don't work. There are many fad diets to choose from.

At the end of the 1800s, a man named Horace Fletcher created a diet called *Fletcherism*. According to Fletcher, people should chew[1] each piece of food 32 times. Fletcher thought all this chewing helped people lose weight and become healthier Why did Fletcher decide on the number 32? It was only because most people have 32 teeth! Fletcher gave other advice about eating, too. For example, he said that people shouldn't eat when they are angry or sad.

Fletcher wore a white jacket to look like a doctor But he had no formal education in medicine, nutrition, or health. People had no reason to follow his advice. But they did. They listened to his speeches all over the country, and they tried his diet. Fletcherism was popular for many years, and Horace Fletcher became a rich man. That's because some people will try anything to lose weight!

[1]chew: to break food into small pieces by moving the teeth up and down

3. Answer the QUESTIONS FOR PAIR A together.

QUESTIONS FOR PAIR A

    a. When was Fletcherism popular?

    _____

    b. What was Horace Fletcher's advice about eating?

    _____

    c. What medical education did Fletcher have?

    _____

4. Find a Pair B with page 75. Answer their questions about your article.

5. Ask them the QUESTIONS TO ASK PAIR B. Write their answers.

QUESTIONS TO ASK PAIR B

    a. How often do people on the Cabbage Soup Diet eat cabbage soup?

    _____

    b. Why does the Cabbage Soup Diet sometimes work?

    _____

    c. What can happen when people stay on the diet for more than 7 days?

    _____

> **KEEP GOING!**
> Talk about diets. What is the most interesting diet you've ever heard of? Does it work?

Pair B: Fad Diets

1. Find a partner who has page 75. You are Pair B.

2. Read the article.

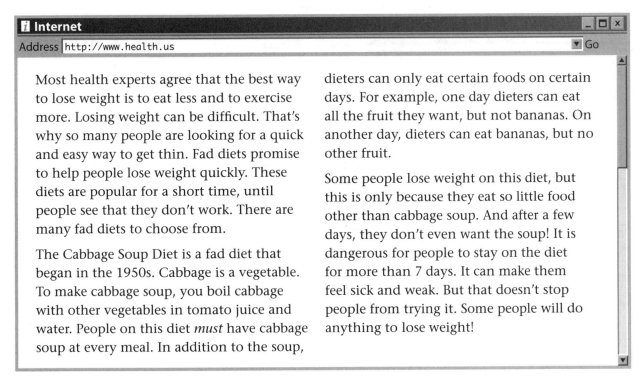

Most health experts agree that the best way to lose weight is to eat less and to exercise more. Losing weight can be difficult. That's why so many people are looking for a quick and easy way to get thin. Fad diets promise to help people lose weight quickly. These diets are popular for a short time, until people see that they don't work. There are many fad diets to choose from.

The Cabbage Soup Diet is a fad diet that began in the 1950s. Cabbage is a vegetable. To make cabbage soup, you boil cabbage with other vegetables in tomato juice and water. People on this diet *must* have cabbage soup at every meal. In addition to the soup,

dieters can only eat certain foods on certain days. For example, one day dieters can eat all the fruit they want, but not bananas. On another day, dieters can eat bananas, but no other fruit.

Some people lose weight on this diet, but this is only because they eat so little food other than cabbage soup. And after a few days, they don't even want the soup! It is dangerous for people to stay on the diet for more than 7 days. It can make them feel sick and weak. But that doesn't stop people from trying it. Some people will do anything to lose weight!

3. Answer the QUESTIONS FOR PAIR B together.

QUESTIONS FOR PAIR B

a. How often do people on the Cabbage Soup Diet eat cabbage soup?

_____

b. Why does the Cabbage Soup Diet sometimes work?

_____

c. What can happen when people stay on the diet for more than 7 days?

_____

4. Find a Pair A with page 74. Ask them the QUESTIONS TO ASK PAIR A. Write their answers.

QUESTIONS TO ASK PAIR A

a. When was Fletcherism popular?

_____

b. What was Horace Fletcher's advice about eating?

_____

c. What medical education did Fletcher have?

_____

5. Answer Pair A's questions about your article.

> **KEEP GOING!**
> Talk about diets. What is the most interesting diet you've ever heard of? Does it work?

The Chef Presents

The Project: Write a recipe and present it on your own cooking show
Supplies: notebook paper, pens, large index cards, or use a word processing program
(if computers are available); pots, pans, and cooking tools (optional)
Resources: dictionaries, cookbooks

1. Work with 3–5 students. Introduce yourself.

2. Choose your job.

> **Leader:** Help your team work together and watch the time.
> **Recorder:** Write the team's ideas.
> **Supplier:** Get the supplies and the resources.
> **Actor:** Act out cooking the recipe.
> **Researcher:** Find information to help your team complete the project.
> **Reporter:** Read the script for your team's cooking show.

3. Brainstorm ideas about a dish you like to cook. What ingredients do you need?
   How do you cook the dish?

> **Leader** Give the team 10 minutes. Ask each person the questions.
> **Recorder:** Write the name and answers of each team member.

4. Write the recipe and plan the cooking show.

> **Supplier:** Get the supplies and the resources from your teacher.
> **Team** Choose one idea for a dish and write the recipe. Decide on a name for your cooking show.
> Write the script to explain each step of the recipe.
> **Reporter:** Practice reading the script.
> **Actor:** Practice acting out the script.
> **Researcher:** Use a dictionary and cookbooks to help your team with vocabulary and spelling.

5. Show your project to the class.

> **Reporter:** Introduce the show to the class and read the script.
> **Actor:** Act out the steps of the recipe.

KEEP GOING!

If possible, make a copy of your recipe for each student. Choose one of the recipes to try
at home. Report back to your class on the results!

Unit 7 Money Wise

Picture A: Millionaire Man

1. Find a partner who has Picture B (page 79).

2. Work with your partner to find 10 differences between your pictures.

3. Write the picture differences in the chart below.

	Picture A	**Picture B**
1.	*The man won $1,000,000.*	*The man won $5,000,000.*
2.		
3.		
4.		
5.		
6.		
7.		
8.		
9.		
10.		

KEEP GOING!

Talk about the last time you were in a bank. What did you do there?

Picture B: Millionaire Man

1. Find a partner with Picture A (page 78)

2. Work with your partner to find 10 differences between your pictures.

B

3. Write the picture differences in the chart below.

	Picture A	Picture B
1.	The man won $1,000,000.	The man won $5,000,000.
2.		
3.		
4.		
5.		
6.		
7.		
8.		
9.		
10.		

KEEP GOING!
Talk about the last time you were in a bank. What did you do there?

Every Penny Counts

1. Work with 3 classmates.
2. Look at the picture. Read the first sentence.
3. Take turns writing 1 sentence about the picture. Write as many as you can.
4. Check your spelling in a dictionary.

Mark wants to save money to buy the computer of his dreams.

_____

_____

_____

_____

_____

_____

_____

_____

KEEP GOING!
Choose a Reporter. Have the Reporter read your 3 most interesting sentences to the class.

A Smart Plan

Partner A
• **Read a sentence to Partner B.** • **Listen to Partner B repeat the sentence.**   **Is it correct? If not, say it again.**
1. Will Alan save money if he takes the bus to work every day? 2. If he takes the bus, he won't save any money. 3. How much money will he save if he walks to work? 4. If he walks to work, he'll save $650.00 by the end of the year.
• **Listen to Partner B say a sentence.** • **Repeat the sentence.** • **Write the sentence.**
5.
6.
7.
8.

------------------------------ FOLD HERE ------------------------------

Partner B
• **Listen to Partner A say a sentence.** • **Repeat the sentence.** • **Write the sentence.**
1.
2.
3.
4.
• **Read a sentence to Partner A.** • **Listen to Partner A repeat the sentence.**   **Is it correct? If not, say it again.**
5. If Alan saves $650.00, what will he buy with it? 6. If he saves $650.00, he'll buy a used car. 7. If he buys a car, what will he do with it? 8. If he buys a car, he'll drive to work!

KEEP GOING!

Write 5 sentences about your plans to save and spend money. Talk about your sentences with a partner.

If I make coffee at home, I won't spend money at the coffee shop.

Spending Free Time

1. Read the questions. Write your answers in the chart.
2. Ask your classmates the questions in the chart.
3. Write your classmates' names and answers in the chart.
4. Use complete sentences to answer your classmates' questions.

If you have some free time this weekend will you . . .	My answers	_____'s answers	_____'s answers	_____'s answers
go shopping?				
visit friends?				
clean your home?				
see a movie?				
cook a special meal?				
read a book?				

5. Work with a partner. Compare your charts. Write 6 sentences.

Many students will see a movie if they have free time this weekend.

1. _____
2. _____
3. _____
4. _____
5. _____
6. _____

KEEP GOING!

Is it more important to relax or do housework during your free time? Why? Talk about your opinions with the class.

Billing Mistakes?

1. Work with 2 classmates. Say all the lines in the script.

2. Choose your character.

3. Finish the conversation. Write more lines for each character.

4. Practice the lines.

5. Act out the role-play with your group.

Scene	Characters	Props
A phone call	• Customer Service Manager • Parent • Teenager	Two telephones or cell phones

The Script

Customer Service Manager: Branson Credit Card. How can I help you?

Parent: I'm calling about a problem on my credit card bill.

Customer Service Manager: What seems to be the problem?

Parent: Well, there are a few charges on the bill that aren't mine.

Customer Service Manager: Can you give me an example?

Parent: First, there's a charge for $25 from a store called Mike's Music.

Teenager: Umm. I have to tell you something.

Parent: Ssh...I'm on the phone.

Teenager: But...umm...I bought some CDs with your credit card.

Parent: What?! We'll talk about this when I get off the phone.

Customer Service Manager: What are the other charges you're calling about?

KEEP GOING!

Watch your classmates' role-plays. Write the answers to these questions: What other charges do the people talk about? Are these charges mistakes on the bill?

Pair A: Your Money and Your Life

1. Find a partner with page 84. You are Pair A.

2. Read the article.

People often say that "opposites attract." For example, in some couples, one person is quiet, while the other person talks a lot. One person likes to go out, and the other likes to stay home. And sometimes one person likes to save money and the other prefers to spend it. This is true for Mike and Maria Hart. The Harts are happy together But when it comes to money, they just can't agree.

Maria is a saver. She thinks you should always save money because you never know when you might need it. When Maria has extra money, she puts it into a savings account. She always takes a shopping list to the supermarket, and she only buys what's on it. And she always looks for the best prices.

Mike thinks his wife is great with money, but sometimes her attitude upsets him. "She's too worried about money," Mike says. "For example, last week we had dinner at a nice restaurant. Did she enjoy the meal? No. She spent the whole time talking about how expensive it was. It gave me heartburn It's not healthy to worry about money so much."

People like Maria are smart to be careful about money, but Mike is right, too. Worrying too much about money can prevent you from enjoying some of the wonderful things in life.

3. Answer the QUESTIONS FOR PAIR A together.

QUESTIONS FOR PAIR A

   a. What does Maria do when she has extra money?

_____

   b. What are two ways Maria saves money?

_____

   c. Why does her attitude about money sometimes upset Mike?

_____

4. Find a pair B with page 85. Answer their questions about your article.

5. Ask them the QUESTIONS TO ASK PAIR B. Write their answers.

QUESTIONS TO ASK PAIR B

   a. What does Mike want to do with extra money?

_____

   b. What does Mike like to spend money on?

_____

   c. Why does his attitude about money sometimes upset Maria?

_____

> **KEEP GOING!**
> Talk about saving and spending money. Are you a saver or a spender? Give some examples.

Pair B: Your Money and Your Life

1. Find a partner with page 85. You are Pair B.

2. Read the article.

People often say that "opposites attract." For example, in some couples, one person is quiet, while the other person talks a lot. One person likes to go out, and the other likes to stay home. And sometimes one person likes to save money and the other prefers to spend it. This is true for Mike and Maria Hart. The Harts are happy together. But when it comes to money, they just can't agree.

Mike is a spender. If there is any extra money at the end of the month, Mike wants to have fun. He likes to shop for clothes, CDs, and computer equipment. He doesn't think twice about buying expensive coffee on his way to work or taking a taxi instead of walking home. Mike wants to enjoy life with the money he earns.

Maria understands how Mike feels, but sometimes his attitude about money upsets her. "Last week I came home and found a big screen TV!" says Maria. "We never talked about buying it. I'm afraid to ask how much he paid for it. If Mike keeps spending money like this, we won't be able to retire until we're 99!"

People like Mike know how to enjoy life. That's very important, but Maria is right, too. Spending money without giving any thought to saving could create big problems in the future.

3. Answer the QUESTIONS FOR PAIR B together.

QUESTIONS FOR PAIR B

a. What does Mike want to do with extra money?

_____

b. What does Mike like to spend money on?

_____

c. Why does his attitude about money sometimes upset Maria?

_____

4. Find a Pair A that has page 84. Ask them the QUESTIONS TO ASK PAIR A. Write their answers.

QUESTIONS TO ASK PAIR A

a. What does Maria do when she has extra money?

_____

b. What are two ways Maria saves money?

_____

c. Why does her attitude about money sometimes upset Mike?

_____

5. Answer Pair A's questions about your article.

KEEP GOING!
Talk about saving and spending money. Are you a saver or a spender? Give some examples.

Save Money for a Trip

The Project: Choose a place for a team trip, and write a list of ways to save money for the trip
Supplies: notebook paper and pens, or a use word processing program (if computers available)
Resources: dictionaries, travel sections of newspapers or magazines, travel brochures, or websites

	Ways to Save Money for Our Trip to Funland, U.S.A.	
O	1. Bring our lunches to school.	6.
	2. Don't buy books. Read library books.	7.
	3.	8.
	4.	9.
	5.	10.

1. Work with 3–5 students. Introduce yourself.

2. Choose your job.

>**Leader:** Help your team work together and watch the time.
>**Recorder:** Write the team's ideas.
>**Supplier:** Get the supplies and the resources.
>**Researcher:** Find information to help your team complete the project.
>**Reporter:** Tell the class about the project.

3. Brainstorm answers to these questions: Where would you like to go on a team trip? What are some ways to save money for the trip?

>**Leader:** Give the team 5 minutes. Ask each person the questions.
>**Recorder:** Write the name and answers of each team member.

4. Choose the place and write the list.

>**Supplier:** Get the supplies and the resources from your teacher.
>**Recorder:** At the top of the page, write: *Ways to Save Money for Our Trip to* _____.
>**Researcher:** Find information to help your team decide on a place to visit.
>**Team:**
>- Choose a place to visit, and write it in the space at the top of the page.
>- Make a list of 8–10 ways to save money for your team trip.
>- Help the Reporter plan a class presentation.

5. Show your project to the class.

>**Reporter:** Tell the class about the place your team chose and your 3 best ideas for saving money.

KEEP GOING!

Which team has the best plan for saving money for their trip?
Talk about your opinions.

Unit 8 Living Well

Picture A: Inside a Hospital

1. Find a partner with Picture B (page 89).

2. Work with your partner to find 10 differences between your pictures.

3. Write the picture differences in the chart below.

	Picture A	**Picture B**
1.	*Pediatrics is on the left side of the second floor.*	*Maternity is on the left side of the second floor.*
2.		
3.		
4.		
5.		
6.		
7.		
8.		
9.		
10.		

KEEP GOING!

Talk about the different reasons people go to a hospital. What kinds of things happen at a hospital?

Picture B: Inside a Hospital

1. Find a partner with Picture A (page 88).

2. Work with your partner to find 10 differences between your pictures.

3. Write the picture differences in the chart below.

	Picture A	Picture B
1.	*Pediatrics is on the left side of the second floor.*	*Maternity is on the left side of the second floor.*
2.		
3.		
4.		
5.		
6.		
7.		
8.		
9.		
10.		

KEEP GOING!

Talk about the different reasons people go to a hospital. What kinds of things happen at a hospital?

The Odd Couple

1. Work with 3 classmates.

2. Look at the picture. Read the first sentence.

3. Take turns writing 1 sentence about the picture. Write as many sentences as you can.

4. Check your spelling in a dictionary.

Sara Brown thinks her husband Sam has too many unhealthy habits.

_____

_____

_____

_____

_____

_____

_____

_____

KEEP GOING!

Choose a Reporter. Have the Reporter read your 3 most interesting sentences to the class.

Habits and Health

Partner A
• **Read a sentence to Partner B.** • **Listen to Partner B repeat the sentence. Is it correct? If not, say it again.**
1. Did Tom use to have any health problems? 2. Yes, he did. 3. What kind of health problems did he have? 4. He used to feel tired and nervous all of the time.
• **Listen to Partner B say a sentence.** • **Repeat the sentence.** • **Write the sentence.**
5.
6.
7.
8.

- FOLD HERE -

Partner B
• **Listen to Partner A say a sentence.** • **Repeat the sentence.** • **Write the sentence.**
1.
2.
3.
4.
• **Read a sentence to Partner A.** • **Listen to Partner A repeat the sentence. Is it correct? If not, say it again.**
5. Why did Tom use to feel terrible all the time? 6. He used to sit around and watch a lot of television. 7. He didn't use to exercise at all. 8. He used to eat fast food at every meal.

KEEP GOING!

Write 5 sentences about habits you used to have. Talk about your sentences with a partner.
I used to eat a lot of cookies and candy.

When You Were a Child

1. Read the questions. Write your answers in the chart.

2. Ask your classmates the questions in the chart.

3. Write your classmates' names and answers in the chart.

4. Use complete sentences to answer your classmates' questions.

When you were a child, . . .	My answers	_____'s answers	_____'s answers	_____'s answers
did you use to like school?				
did you use to have many friends?				
did you use to live in a small town?				
did you use to get sick often?				
what did you use to like to eat?				
what did you use to do on the weekends?				

5. Work with a partner. Compare your charts. Write 6 sentences.

Elena and I used to like school when we were children, but John didn't.

1. _____
2. _____
3. _____
4. _____
5. _____
6. _____

KEEP GOING!

What is the best thing you remember about your childhood? Talk about your opinions with the class.

Sleep Suggestions

1. Work with 2 classmates. Say all the lines in the script.

2. Choose your character.

3. Finish the conversation. Write more lines for each character.

4. Practice the lines.

5. Act out the role-play with your group.

Scene	Characters	Props
A doctor's office	• Patient • Doctor • Nurse	• Books • Notebooks • Papers

The Script

Patient: I haven't been sleeping well, Doctor.

Doctor: Is this a new problem?

Patient: Yes, it is. I used to sleep really well.

Doctor: Have you been under a lot of stress lately?

Patient: I guess so. I've been studying morning, noon, and night.

Doctor: Why don't you take some time to relax before you go to sleep?

Patient: OK, I can do that.

Nurse: I have a few suggestions, too.

Patient: Yes?

Nurse: You could take a hot bath before you get into bed.

Patient: Good idea. I'll give it a try.

KEEP GOING!

Watch your classmates' role-plays. Write the answers to these questions: What other suggestions do the doctor and nurse give the patient? What is the patient going to do?

Pair A: The Best Medicine

1. Find a partner with page 94. You are Pair A.

2. Read the article.

You probably know that to stay healthy you should exercise, eat healthy foods, and get enough sleep. But you may not know about something else you can do. It's free, it's easy, and you can do it almost anywhere at any time. What is it? Just laugh! Many studies have shown that laughing is good for your health.

Hospitals across the U.S. are using laughter as a tool to help sick patients. Doctors have found that laughter decreases pain, relaxes people, and helps them get better. Hospitals bring laughter to their patients in different ways. Some hospitals show their patients funny videos. Some children's hospitals invite circus clowns to entertain their patients. The children laugh at the clowns' big feet, red noses, and funny actions. One program, the Big Apple Circus Clown Care Unit, has 93 clowns. They visit about 200,000 sick children each year in 17 hospitals around the country. Marisol Reyes, a nurse at one of the largest children's hospitals in the U.S., says, "You see the children's faces light up when the clowns come in. And you can actually see their pain go away."

No wonder people often say, "Laughter is the best medicine!"

3. Answer the QUESTIONS FOR PAIR A together.

QUESTIONS FOR PAIR A

   a. How does laughter help patients in hospitals?

   _____

   b. What are two ways hospitals bring laughter to their patients?

   _____

   c. What does Marisol Reyes say about the hospital clowns?

   _____

4. Find a Pair B with page 95. Answer their questions about your article.

5. Ask them the QUESTIONS TO ASK PAIR B. Write their answers.

QUESTIONS TO ASK PAIR B

   a. What happens when employees feel stress?

   _____

   b. How may laughter help employees?

   _____

   c. How has Ben Cole brought more laughter to his office?

   _____

KEEP GOING!
Talk about laughter. What makes you laugh? How do you feel when you laugh?

Pair B: The Best Medicine

1. Find a partner with page 95. You are Pair B.

2. Read the article.

You probably know that to stay healthy you should exercise, eat healthy foods, and get enough sleep. But you may not know about something else you can do. It's free, it's easy, and you can do it almost anywhere at any time. What is it? Just laugh! Many studies have shown that laughing is good for your health.

Workplaces across the U.S. are using laughter as a way to manage employee stress. When people feel stress, they get tired easily, and they are more likely to get sick. Stressed employees take more sick days and are less efficient workers. Researchers have found that laughter may help employees lower stress and prevent illness.

Companies are trying different ways to bring laughter into the workplace. For example, Ben Cole, an office manager in a large company, says, "I bring softballs for my employees to play with at break time. We start meetings with a funny story or joke, and we hang up funny pictures every day. There's a lot of laughter in our office now. Our employees seem happier and healthier. They almost never take sick days. Coming to work is too much fun!"

No wonder people often say, "Laughter is the best medicine!"

3. Answer the QUESTIONS FOR PAIR B together.

QUESTIONS FOR PAIR B

   a. What happens when employees feel stress?

   _____

   b. How may laughter help employees?

   _____

   c. How has Ben Cole brought more laughter to his office?

   _____

4. Find a Pair A with page 94. Ask them the QUESTIONS TO ASK PAIR A. Write their answers.

QUESTIONS TO ASK PAIR A

   a. How does laughter help patients in hospitals?

   _____

   b. What are two ways hospitals bring laughter to their patients?

   _____

   c. What does Marisol Reyes say about the hospital clowns?

   _____

5. Answer Pair A's questions about your article.

KEEP GOING!

Talk about laughter. What makes you laugh? How do you feel when you laugh?

How Healthy Are You?

The Project: Create a health survey
Supplies: notebook paper and pens, or use a word processor (if computers are available)
Resources: dictionaries

Health Survey

I drink a lot of soda.	Yes	No
I eat a lot of fast food.	Yes	No
I watch 2 or more hours of TV every day.	Yes	No

1. Work with 3–5 students. Introduce yourself.

2. Choose your job.

> **Leader:** Help your team work together and watch the time.
> **Recorder:** Write the team's ideas.
> **Supplier:** Get the supplies and the resources.
> **Researcher:** Find information to help your team complete the project.
> **Reporter:** Tell the class about the project.

3. Brainstorm answers to these questions: What are some healthy habits? What are some unhealthy habits?

> **Leader:** Give the team 5 minutes. Ask each person the questions.
> **Recorder:** Write the name and answers of each team member.

4. Create the survey.

> **Supplier:** Get the supplies and resources from your teacher.
> **Team:**
> • Write a list of 8–10 sentences about health habits.
> • Number the sentences and write *Yes* and *No* next to each one.
> • If possible, make copies of your survey for your classmates.
> **Researcher:** Use a dictionary to help your team with vocabulary and spelling.

5. Show your project to the class.

> **Reporter:** Give your survey to another team to complete. Ask them the questions or give them a copy.

KEEP GOING!

After another team has completed your survey, look at their answers.
Talk about the results with your team.

Unit 9 Hit the Road

Picture A: You're Going to Love This Car!

1. Find a partner with Picture B (page 99).

2. Work with your partner to find 10 differences between your pictures.

3. Write the picture differences in the chart below.

	Picture A	Picture B
1.	*The key is in the ignition.*	*The key isn't in the ignition.*
2.		
3.		
4.		
5.		
6.		
7.		
8.		
9.		
10.		

KEEP GOING!

Talk about the parts of a car. What are important things to check before you buy a car?

Picture B: You're Going to Love This Car!

1. Find a partner with Picture A (page 98).

2. Work with your partner to find 10 differences between your pictures.

3. Write the picture differences in the chart below.

	Picture A	**Picture B**
1.	*The key is in the ignition.*	*The key isn't in the ignition.*
2.		
3.		
4.		
5.		
6.		
7.		
8.		
9.		
10.		

KEEP GOING!

Talk about the parts of a car. What are important things to check before you buy a car?

Family Trip

1. Work with 3 classmates.

2. Look at the picture. Read the first sentence.

3. Take turns writing 1 sentence about the picture. Write as many as you can.

4. Check your spelling in a dictionary.

The Santana family took a road trip last summer, and they have many stories to tell.

_____

_____

_____

_____

_____

_____

_____

_____

_____

KEEP GOING!

Choose a Reporter. Have the Reporter read your 3 most interesting sentences to the class.

It Looked Good When I Bought It

Partner A
• **Read a sentence to Partner B.** • **Listen to Partner B repeat the sentence.**   **Is it correct? If not, say it again.**
1. The car looked good when I bought it. 2. The problems started when I brought it home. 3. When I got out of the car, the door fell off. 4. When I looked under the hood, I saw smoke.
• **Listen to Partner B say a sentence.** • **Repeat the sentence.** • **Write the sentence.**
5.
6.
7.
8.

- FOLD HERE -

Partner B
• **Listen to Partner A say a sentence.** • **Repeat the sentence.** • **Write the sentence.**
1.
2.
3.
4.
• **Read a sentence to Partner A.** • **Listen to Partner A repeat the sentence.**   **Is it correct? If not, say it again.**
5. Now when I start the car, it makes a strange noise. 6. When I wash the car, water gets into the gas tank. 7. I'm sure there will be new problems when I drive it tomorrow. 8. I'll be more careful when I buy my next car.

KEEP GOING!

Work with a partner. Write 5 sentences about possible problems with a car.
When I drive the car, it leaks oil.

I Need a Vacation!

1. Read the questions. Write your answers in the chart.
2. Ask your classmates the questions in the chart.
3. Write your classmates' names and answers in the chart.
4. Use complete sentences to answer your classmates' questions.

Ask and answer these questions.	My answers	_____'s answers	_____'s answers	_____'s answers
Will you take a vacation after you finish school this year?				
Before you take a trip, what is one thing you do to prepare?				
What is the last thing you do before you leave on a trip?				
What is one thing you like to do when you are on vacation?				
What is the first thing you usually do when you get home from a trip?				

5. Work with a partner. Compare your charts. Write 6 sentences.

   I buy a map before I take a trip, but Yuri checks maps on the Internet.

1. _____
2. _____
3. _____
4. _____
5. _____
6. _____

KEEP GOING!
Describe the vacation of your dreams. Talk about your opinions with your class.

Car for Sale

1. Work with 3 classmates. Say all the lines in the script.

2. Choose your character.

3. Finish the conversation. Write more lines for each character.

4. Practice the lines.

5. Act out the role-play with your group.

Scene	**Characters**	**Props**
A driveway	• Buyer 1 • Buyer 2 • Seller 1 • Seller 2	A newspaper

The Script

Buyer 1: Hi.

Buyer 2: We're here to look at the car you advertised in the newspaper.

Seller 1: Great!

Seller 2: Thanks for coming. The car is right here.

Buyer 1: Are there any problems we should know about?

Seller 2: Well, the headlights don't work, and the right turn signal doesn't either.

Buyer 2: The car looks kind of old. $8,000 seems like a lot of money for it.

Seller 1: Well, I'm sure we can work something out.

Seller 2: I'm sure we can make a deal.

Buyer 2: Are there any other problems with the car?

KEEP GOING!

Watch your classmates' role-plays. Write the answers to these questions: What other problems does the car have? Do the people decide to buy the car?

Pair A: New Car or Used Car?

1. Find a partner with page 104. You are Pair A.

2. Read the article.

People in the U.S. buy about 62 million cars a year. About two thirds of these cars are used, and the others are new. Choosing between a new car and a used car is not easy. There are many things to think about before you make a decision.

We asked buyers of new cars to tell us the reasons for their purchases. People said that the maintenance of a new car usually doesn't cost a lot for the first few years. During this time, the car probably will not need new tires or a battery. People also said that new cars are more reliable than used cars—there are usually fewer problems on the road. If there are problems with any of the parts during the first year or two, the car company usually will replace the part. Finally, new car buyers liked the big choice of cars they had. They could get exactly the kind of car they wanted in the color of their choice. And they could get all the newest equipment and technology.

New car buyer Anya Silzoff said, "No used car had everything I wanted. But my beautiful new car has it all! It's a great color, it's safe, it's comfortable, and it even has travel directions on computer!" For people like Anya, new cars are definitely the answer!

3. Answer the QUESTIONS FOR PAIR A together.

QUESTIONS FOR PAIR A

    a. Why are new cars usually less expensive to maintain?

_____

    b. What are two other reasons to buy a new car?

_____

    c. What does Anya Silzoff like about her car?

_____

4. Find a Pair B with page 105. Answer their questions about your article.

5. Ask them the QUESTIONS TO ASK PAIR B. Write their answers.

QUESTIONS TO ASK PAIR B

    a. What is the average price of a new car?

_____

    b. What are two reasons for buying a used car?

_____

    c. What does John Rand think about not having a CD player?

_____

KEEP GOING!

Talk about new cars and used cars. Which kind of car would you like to buy? Why?

Pair B: New Car or Used Car?

1. Find a partner with page 105. You are Pair B.

2. Read the article.

People in the U.S. buy about 62 million cars a year. About two thirds of these cars are used, and the others are new. Choosing between a new car and a used car is not easy. There are many things to think about before you make a decision.

We asked buyers of used cars to tell us the reasons for their purchases. People said that the average price of a new car, $20,000, is just too expensive. Used cars cost much less. People also said that when you buy a used car, you usually can get a bigger car and a better one, too. For example, the least expensive new cars cost about $10,000. New cars that cost $10,000 are often very small. For the same $10,000, you can usually buy a three- or four-year-old car that is larger and more comfortable. You may not have a big choice in the kind of car or the color. And used cars may not have the newest technology that new cars have. But these things were not problems for most used car buyers.

"It's true that my car doesn't have a CD player," said John Rand, a used car buyer. "But it has a radio, and that's all I need." For people like John, used cars are definitely the answer.

3. Answer the QUESTIONS FOR PAIR B together.

QUESTIONS FOR PAIR B

a. What is the average price of a new car?

_____

b. What are two reasons for buying a used car?

_____

c. What does John Rand think about not having a CD player?

_____

4. Find a Pair A with page 104. Ask them the QUESTIONS TO ASK PAIR A. Write their answers.

QUESTIONS TO ASK PAIR A

a. Why are new cars usually less expensive to maintain?

_____

b. What are two other reasons to buy a new car?

_____

c. What does Anya Silzoff like about her car?

_____

5. Answer Pair A's questions about your article.

KEEP GOING!
Talk about new cars and used cars. Which kind of car would you like to buy? Why?

The Perfect Car

The Project: Design a new car and create an ad for it
Supplies: poster board, markers, colored pencils, and crayons
Resources: dictionaries

The Jupiter 500
Comfort, Beauty, and Speed!

The Jupiter 500 is a great car with a beautiful interior for a fantastic price. With an amazing warranty, this is THE car for the stylish customer.

1. Work with 3–5 students. Introduce yourself.

2. Choose your job.

> **Leader:** Help your group work together and watch the time.
> **Recorder:** Write the team's ideas.
> **Supplier:** Get the supplies and the resources.
> **Artist:** Draw the picture.
> **Reporter:** Tell the class about the project.
> **Researcher:** Find information to help your team complete the project.

3. Brainstorm answers to these questions: What does the perfect car look like? What is special about it?

> **Leader:** Give the team 5 minutes. Ask each person the questions.
> **Recorder:** Write the name and answers of each team member.

4. Design the car and create the ad.

> **Team:**
> • Decide on the things that will make your car special.
> • Write an ad for your car.
> • Include a paragraph describing the car.
> **Artist:** Draw the car that your team describes and include the picture in the ad.
> **Researcher:** Use a dictionary to help your team with vocabulary and spelling.

5. Show your project to the class.

> **Reporter:** Show the class your ad and tell them about the car.

KEEP GOING!
Compare all the teams' ads. Decide on which car you would like to buy. Explain why.

Unit 10 Crime Doesn't Pay

Picture A: From Crime to Courtroom

1. Find a partner with Picture B (page 109).

2. Work with your partner to find 10 differences between your pictures.

3. Write the picture differences in the chart below.

	Picture A	**Picture B**
1.	*An older couple is witnessing a crime.*	*A young couple is witnessing a crime.*
2.		
3.		
4.		
5.		
6.		
7.		
8.		
9.		
10.		

KEEP GOING!
Talk about crimes. Describe a crime you read about or saw in the movies or on TV.

Picture B: From Crime to Courtroom

1. Find a partner with Picture A (page 108).

2. Work with your partner to find 10 differences between your pictures.

3. Write the picture differences in the chart below.

	Picture A	Picture B
1.	*An older couple is witnessing a crime.*	*A young couple is witnessing a crime.*
2.		
3.		
4.		
5.		
6.		
7.		
8.		
9.		
10.		

KEEP GOING!
Talk about crimes. Describe a crime you read about or saw in the movies or on TV.

Locked Out!

1. Work with 3 classmates.

2. Look at the pictures. Read the first sentence.

3. Take turns writing 1 sentence about the pictures. Write as many as you can.

4. Check your spelling in a dictionary.

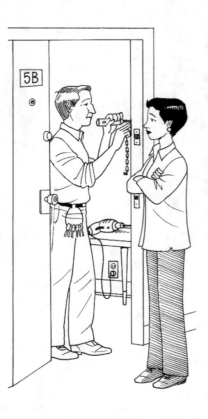

Carmen heard some surprising news about her apartment building, and it worried her.

_____

_____

_____

_____

_____

_____

_____

_____

KEEP GOING!

Choose a Reporter. Have the Reporter read your 3 most interesting sentences to the class.

Staying Safe

Partner A
• **Read a sentence to Partner B.** • **Listen to Partner B repeat the sentence.** **Is it correct? If not, say it again.**
1. Witnessing a crime is scary. 2. Reporting the crime is the right thing to do. 3. Calling 911 quickly is important. 4. Giving clear information about the crime is very helpful.
• **Listen to Partner B say a sentence.** • **Repeat the sentence.** • **Write the sentence.**
5.
6.
7.
8.

- FOLD HERE -

Partner B
• **Listen to Partner A say a sentence.** • **Repeat the sentence.** • **Write the sentence.**
1.
2.
3.
4.
• **Read a sentence to Partner A.** • **Listen to Partner A repeat the sentence.** **Is it correct? If not, say it again.**
5. Walking alone in the dark isn't safe. 6. Beth isn't walking alone tonight. 7. She's walking to the movies with Alan. 8. They're staying in well-lit areas of town.

KEEP GOING!

Write 5 sentences about ways to stay safe. Talk about your sentences with a partner.
Carrying a cell phone with you is a good idea.

Home Security

1. Read the questions. Write your answers in the chart.

2. Ask your classmates the questions in the chart.

3. Write your classmates' names and answers in the chart.

4. Use complete sentences to answer your classmates' questions.

Ask and answer these questions.	My answers	_____'s answers	_____'s answers	_____'s answers
Is having a home in the city safer than having a home in the country?				
Is living in an apartment safer than living in a house?				
Is having a big dog better than having a security alarm?				
Is having a peephole on the front door more important than having a chain lock?				
Is walking alone at night more dangerous than than biking alone at night?				

5. Work with a partner. Compare your charts. Write 6 sentences.

Most people think having a home in the country is safer than having a home in the city.

1. _____

2. _____

3. _____

4. _____

5. _____

6. _____

KEEP GOING!

What are the most important ways to keep your home safe? Talk about your opinions with the class.

Stop That Man!

1. Work with 3 classmates. Say all the lines in the script.
2. Choose your character.
3. Finish the conversation. Write more lines for each character.
4. Practice the lines.
5. Act out the role-play with your group.

Scene

On the street

Characters

• Victim
• Police Officer
• Witness 1
• Witness 2

Props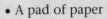

• A pad of paper
• A pen

The Script

Victim: Officer! Officer!

Police Officer: Yes? Is there a problem?

Victim: A man just stole my wallet.

Witness 1: I saw the whole thing.

Witness 2: I tried to stop him, but he ran away.

Police Officer: OK. Tell me what happened. It's important to remember as much as you can.

Victim: I was walking down the street when a man suddenly jumped in front of me.

Witness 1: Then he pushed you down, right?

Victim: Yes!

Police Officer: What happened after that?

KEEP GOING!

Watch your classmates' role-plays. Write the answers to these questions: What happened after the mugger pushed the victim down? Who remembers more about the crime, the victim or the witnesses?

Pair A: Not-So-Smart Criminals

1. Find a partner with page 114. You are Pair A.

2. Read the article.

Some criminals are very smart. They commit crimes so carefully that it is very difficult for the police to find them. In fact, it sometimes takes many years for the police to solve these crimes. However, other criminals are not so smart. They make the job of the police very easy.

One of these easy-to-solve crimes happened in Malaysia. Two robbers broke into a house. They planned to take all the money and valuable things they could find, such as artwork, expensive cameras, and computer equipment. The men worked quickly. They put all the

valuable items into bags. What did the robbers do next? Did they take the bags and leave the house fast? No, they didn't. They decided they were hungry, so they went into the kitchen and made themselves a meal. After eating, the men felt tired, so they decided to lie down for a while. Each man lay down on a sofa, pulled a blanket over himself, and went to sleep. When the owner of the house came home, she found the robbers sleeping. She quickly called the police. The police arrived at the house, woke up the criminals, and arrested them right away!

3. Answer the QUESTIONS FOR PAIR A together.

QUESTIONS FOR PAIR A

   a. What did the robbers plan to take from the house?

   _____

   b. What did they do in the house?

   _____

   c. How did the police catch the robbers?

   _____

4. Find a Pair B with page 115. Answer their questions about your article.

5. Ask them the QUESTIONS TO ASK PAIR B. Write their answers.

QUESTIONS TO ASK PAIR B

   a. From where did the man steal the car?

   _____

   b. Why did the man think he was lucky at first?

   _____

   c. How did the police catch the man?

   _____

> **KEEP GOING!**
> Tell your class a funny crime story you know, or make one up.

Pair B: Not-So-Smart Criminals

1. Find a partner with page 115. You are Pair B.

2. Read the article.

Some criminals are very smart. They commit crimes so carefully that it is very difficult for the police to find them. In fact it sometimes takes many years for the police to solve these crimes. However, other criminals are not so smart. They make the job of the police very easy.

One of these easy-to-solve crimes happened in Russia. A man tried to steal a car from a garage near his house. The man watched the garage all day. He saw the mechanics fixing a car that he really liked. At 6 p.m. the garage closed for the day, and the mechanics went home. The man walked up to his favorite car, and he couldn't believe his luck. The keys were in the ignition! Nobody saw him when he got into the car and drove away. But when he came to a traffic light, he noticed a problem. The car had no brakes! He couldn't stop the car! He drove right through a red light and hit another car. A police car quickly arrived at the accident. The police officer found a stolen car and a criminal with a very red face!

3. Answer the QUESTIONS FOR PAIR B together.

QUESTIONS FOR PAIR B

    a. From where did the man steal the car?

    _____

    b. Why did the man think he was lucky at first?

    _____

    c. How did the police catch the man?

    _____

4. Find a Pair A with page 114. Ask them the QUESTIONS TO ASK PAIR A. Write their answers.

QUESTIONS TO ASK PAIR A

    a. What did the robbers plan to take from the house?

    _____

    b. What did they do in the house?

    _____

    c. How did the police catch the robbers?

    _____

5. Answer Pair A's questions about your article.

KEEP GOING!
Tell your class a funny crime story you know, or make one up.

Safety Tips

The Project: Create a class handbook of safety advice
Supplies: construction paper, notebook paper, magazines, a stapler, glue, pens and colored pencils, or use a word processing program (if computers are available)
Resources: dictionaries, telephone books, emergency number lists, safety brochures, or information from the Internet

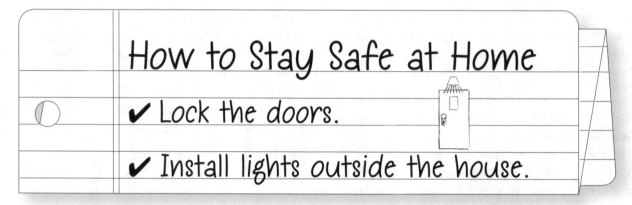

1. Work with 3–5 students. Introduce yourself.

2. Choose your job.

> **Leader:** Help your team work together and watch the time.
> **Recorder:** Write the team's ideas.
> **Supplier:** Get the supplies and the resources.
> **Researcher:** Find information to help your team complete the project.
> **Reporter:** Tell the class about the project.

3. As a team, choose a place for your safety tips: at home, on the street, on public transportation, on the Internet, or another place of your choice.

4. Brainstorm safety tips for your place.

> **Leader:** Give the team 5 minutes. Ask each person for 1 safety tip.
> **Recorder:** Write the name and idea of each team member.
> **Researcher:** Find more safety information for your place. Talk about the information with your team.

5. Write your section of the handbook.

> **Supplier:** Get the supplies and the resources from your teacher.
> **Recorder:** Write *How to Stay Safe* _____ at the top of the page, and complete the title with your place.
> **Team:** Write as many safety tips for your section as you can. Draw or cut out pictures to help explain the information. Help the Reporter plan a class presentation.

6. Show your project to the class.

> **Reporter:** Tell the class about the information in your section.
> **Team:** Help the Reporter. Show pictures and act out some of the information.

KEEP GOING!

Put all the teams' sections together to create a class handbook of safety tips.
Make a cover and a list of the sections.

Unit 11 That's Life

Picture A: Family Pictures

1. Find a partner with Picture B (page 119).

2. Work with your partner to find 10 differences between your pictures.

3. Write the picture differences in the chart below.

	Picture A	**Picture B**
1.	*Julia was born on June 15th.*	*Julia was born on December 9th.*
2.		
3.		
4.		
5.		
6.		
7.		
8.		
9.		
10.		

KEEP GOING!

Talk about life events. What are the important events in your life that have happened so far?

Picture B: Family Pictures

1. Find a partner with Picture A (page 118).

2. Work with your partner to find 10 differences between your pictures.

3. Write the picture differences in the chart below.

	Picture A	Picture B
1.	*Julia was born on June 15th.*	*Julia was born on December 9th.*
2.		
3.		
4.		
5.		
6.		
7.		
8.		
9.		
10.		

KEEP GOING!

Talk about important life events. What are the important life events that have happened in your life so far?

Come to My Party!

1. Work with 3 classmates.

2. Look at the picture. Read the first sentence.

3. Take turns writing 1 sentence about the picture. Write as many as you can.

4. Check your spelling in a dictionary.

Sandra invited all her friends to her party, but only some of them can come.

_____

_____

_____

_____

_____

_____

_____

KEEP GOING!

Choose a Reporter. Have the Reporter read your 3 most interesting sentences to the class.

American Weddings

Partner A
• **Read a sentence to Partner B.** • **Listen to Partner B repeat the sentence.**   **Is it correct? If not, say it again.**
1. Invitations are mailed months before a wedding. 2. The wedding is witnessed by family and friends. 3. The bride and groom are congratulated. 4. Many photos are taken of the happy couple.
• **Listen to Partner B say a sentence.** • **Repeat the sentence.** • **Write the sentence.**
5.
6.
7.
8.

- FOLD HERE -

Partner B
• **Listen to Partner A say a sentence.** • **Repeat the sentence.** • **Write the sentence.**
1.
2.
3.
4.
• **Read a sentence to Partner A.** • **Listen to Partner A repeat the sentence.**   **Is it correct? If not, say it again.**
5. A wedding is often followed by a party. 6. Food is served, and music is played. 7. The wedding cake is cut by the bride and groom. 8. The bride and groom are given many presents.

KEEP GOING!

Write 5 sentences about special things you do for life events such as a graduation, the birth of a child, or a funeral. Talk about your sentences with a partner.

In my family, a girl is given a big party on her fifteenth birthday.

Party Time

1. Read the questions. Write your answers in the chart.
2. Ask your classmates the questions in the chart.
3. Write your classmates' names and answers in the chart.
4. Use complete sentences to answer your classmates' questions.

At your favorite parties, . . .	My answers	_____'s answers	_____'s answers	_____'s answers
what kind of food is served?				
who is invited?				
what time are the guests invited to arrive?				
what kind of music is played?				
what kind of clothes are worn?				

5. Work with a partner. Compare your charts. Write 6 sentences.

At my favorite parties, Mexican food is served. At Carla's favorite parties, pizza is served.

1. _____
2. _____
3. _____
4. _____
5. _____
6. _____

KEEP GOING!

What was the best party you ever went to? Why was it such a good party?
Talk about your opinions with the class.

Big News

1. Work with 3 classmates. Say all the lines in the script.

2. Choose your character.

3. Finish the conversation. Write more lines for each character.

4. Practice the lines.

5. Act out the role-play with your group.

Scene	Characters	Props
A restaurant	• Friend 1 • Friend 2 • Friend 3 • Friend 4	A ring

The Script

Friend 1: We have some exciting news.

Friend 2: Are you ready for a surprise?

Friend 3: Sure.

Friend 4: What is it? Tell us!

Friend 1 and Friend 2: We're getting married!

Friend 3: Congratulations! That's great news!

Friend 4: When is the wedding?

Friend 1: January 20. We hope you'll be able to come.

Friend 3: Of course we will!

Friend 4: Hey listen, we have some news for you, too.

KEEP GOING!

Watch your classmates' role-plays. Write the answers to these questions: What news did Friends 3 and 4 want to tell their friends? How did Friends 1 and 2 feel about the news?

Pair A: New Home, New Life

1. Find a partner with page 124. You are Pair A.

2. Read the interview.

Real Lives Weekly: Did you know that the average American moves to a new home 11 times in life? Our reporter recently interviewed people who have changed their lives by moving. They have interesting stories to tell.

Reporter: Last year, Alma Diaz moved from a big city to a small town. Alma, tell us about your life before you moved.

Alma: Sure. Until last year, I lived in New York City. I loved the shops, the restaurants, and the museums. And I had a great job as a chef at a popular restaurant.

Reporter: Why did you move?

Alma: I fell in love! One night I met a wonderful man at the restaurant. He was from Clinton, New York. We talked on the phone every day and visited each other often. We decided to get married, and I moved to Clinton.

Reporter: Was the move hard for you?

Alma: Yes, at first it was. Clinton seemed so quiet. There wasn't much to do. Then one day, a neighbor brought me flowers to welcome me to town. We became good friends. And soon I opened my own restaurant.

Reporter: How do you feel about Clinton now?

Alma: I love it! The people are friendly. I know all my neighbors. And I love my new restaurant. Moving to Clinton was the best thing I've ever done.

3. Answer the QUESTIONS FOR PAIR A together.

QUESTIONS FOR PAIR A

  a. Why did Alma move to Clinton, New York?

  _____

  b. How did Alma feel about the town at first?

  _____

  c. What does Alma like about living in a small town now?

  _____

4. Find a Pair B with page 125. Answer their questions about your article.

5. Ask them the QUESTIONS TO ASK PAIR B. Write their answers.

QUESTIONS TO ASK PAIR B

  a. Why did Mark move to Chicago?

  _____

  b. How did Mark feel about the city at first?

  _____

  c. What does Mark like about living in a big city now?

  _____

> **KEEP GOING!**
> Talk about places to live. Would you rather live in a big city or a small town? Why?

Pair B: New Home, New Life

1. Find a partner with page 125. You are Pair B.

2. Read the interview.

Real Lives Weekly: Did you know that the average American moves to a new home 11 times in life? Our reporter recently interviewed people who have changed their lives by moving. They have interesting stories to tell.

Reporter: Last year, Mark Smith moved from a small town to a big city. Mark, tell us about your life before you moved.

Mark: Sure. Until last year, I lived in Waldron, Arkansas. I enjoyed all the things you can do in a small town. I used to take long walks, swim in a nearby lake, and spend time with old friends.

Reporter: Why did you move to Chicago?

Mark: I went there for college.

Reporter: Was the move hard for you?

Mark: Yes, at first it was. Life was so different! I couldn't get used to the traffic and the noise. The sound of car horns and cell phones never stopped! Everything seemed to move too fast. But little by little, I started to enjoy the city.

Interviewer: How do you feel about Chicago now?

Mark: I think it's exciting. I've met many interesting people. I like the city's energy. It's always busy, and there's always something to do. Sometimes I miss Waldron, but I think I'll stay in Chicago after college and look for a job. It's starting to feel like home here.

3. Answer the QUESTIONS FOR PAIR B together.

QUESTIONS FOR PAIR B

  a. Why did Mark move to Chicago?

  _____

  b. How did Mark feel about the city at first?

  _____

  c. What does Mark like about living in a big city now?

  _____

4. Find a Pair A with page 124. Ask them the QUESTIONS TO ASK PAIR A. Write their answers.

QUESTIONS TO ASK PAIR A

  a. Why did Alma move to Clinton, New York?

  _____

  b. How did Alma feel about the town at first?

  _____

  c. What does Alma like about living in a small town now?

  _____

5. Answer Pair A's questions about your article.

KEEP GOING!
Talk about places to live. Would you rather live in a big city or a small town? Why?

Team Timeline

The Project: Create a timeline that shows important events in the lives of your team members
Supplies: poster board, notebook paper, markers, pens, colored pencils or crayons, tape
Resources: dictionaries

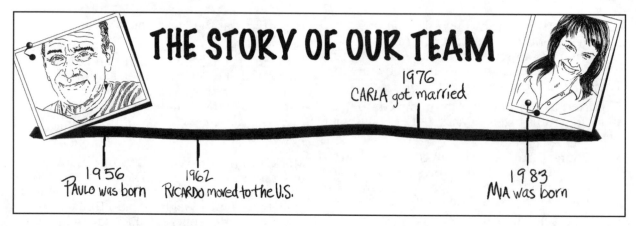

1. Work with 3–5 students. Introduce yourself.

2. Choose your job.

> **Leader:** Help your team work together and watch the time.
> **Recorder:** Write the team's ideas.
> **Supplier:** Get the supplies and the resources.
> **Graphic Designer:** Design the timeline.
> **Reporter:** Tell the class about the project.

3. Brainstorm answers to these questions: What were the most important events of your life so far? When did these events happen?

> **Leader:** Give the team 5 minutes. Ask each person the questions.
> **Recorder:** Write the name and answers of each team member.

4. Create the timeline.

> **Supplier:** Get the supplies and the resources from your teacher.
> **Graphic Designer:** Draw a timeline. Start with the year the oldest person on your team was born. End with the current year. In between, write the years that are important for your team members.
> **Team:**
> • Write the important events in your lives above or below the correct years.
> • Draw a picture of yourself on a separate piece of paper, or take out a photo if you have one.
> • Help the Reporter plan a class presentation.
> **Researcher:** Use a dictionary to help your team with vocabulary and spelling.

5. Show your project to the class.

> **Reporter:** Tell the class about each person on your team's timeline.
> **Team:** As the Reporter talks about your life, add your photo or drawing to the timeline, and point to your important dates.

KEEP GOING!
Invite your classmates to ask questions about the important events in your life.

Unit 12 Do the Right Thing

Picture A: Citizen Rights and Responsibilities

1. Find a partner with Picture B (page 129).

2. Work with your partner to find 10 differences between your pictures.

3. Write the picture differences in the chart below.

	Picture A	Picture B
1.	*The driver is obeying the law.*	*The driver is not obeying the law.*
2.		
3.		
4.		
5.		
6.		
7.		
8.		
9.		
10.		

KEEP GOING!
Talk about the rights and responsibilities of students in your classroom and at your school.

Picture B: Citizen Rights and Responsibilities

1. Find a partner with Picture A (page 128).
2. Work with your partner to find 10 differences between your pictures.

3. Write the picture differences in the chart below.

	Picture A	Picture B
1.	*The driver is obeying the law.*	*The driver is not obeying the law.*
2.		
3.		
4.		
5.		
6.		
7.		
8.		
9.		
10.		

KEEP GOING!
Talk about the rights and responsibilities of students in your classroom and at your school.

Take Action!

1. Work with 3 classmates.

2. Look at the picture. Read the first sentence.

3. Take turns writing 1 sentence about the picture. Write as many as you can.

4. Check your spelling in a dictionary.

The citizens of Upton think it's important to get involved in their community.

_____

_____

_____

_____

_____

_____

_____

_____

KEEP GOING!

Choose a Reporter. Have the Reporter read your 3 most interesting sentences to the class.

Community Volunteers

Partner A
• **Read a sentence to Partner B.** • **Listen to Partner B repeat the sentence.**   **Is it correct? If not, say it again.**
1. Anna wants to volunteer in her community. 2. She doesn't want to work inside a building. 3. She enjoys working outdoors. 4. She plans to volunteer to clean up her local park.
• **Listen to Partner B say a sentence.** • **Repeat the sentence.** • **Write the sentence.**
5.
6.
7.
8.

- FOLD HERE -

Partner B
• **Listen to Partner A say a sentence.** • **Repeat the sentence.** • **Write the sentence.**
1.
2.
3.
4.
• **Read a sentence to Partner A.** • **Listen to Partner A repeat the sentence.**   **Is it correct? If not, say it again.**
5. Sam began volunteering at the senior center this year. 6. He agreed to visit the seniors twice a month. 7. He likes reading and talking to the people there. 8. He will continue to volunteer at the center next year.

KEEP GOING!

Write 5 sentences about things you would like to do in your community. Talk about your sentences with a partner.

I would like to volunteer at the animal shelter.

Plans for the Future

1. Read the questions. Write your answers in the chart.
2. Ask your classmates the questions in the chart.
3. Write your classmates' names and answers in the chart.
4. Use complete sentences to answer your classmates' questions.

Ask and answer these questions.	My answers	_____'s answers	_____'s answers	_____'s answers
Do you plan to look for a job in the next 6 months?				
Do you want to start your own business in the future?				
Will you continue studying English after this class?				
What is one thing you hope to do this summer?				
What is one place you plan to visit in the future?				

5. Work with a partner. Compare your charts. Write 6 sentences.

Miguel and I plan to look for jobs in the next six months, but Boris and Marie don't.

1. _____
2. _____
3. _____
4. _____
5. _____
6. _____

KEEP GOING!

Is it important to make plans for the future? Why or why not?
Talk about your opinions with the class.

We Need Legal Advice

1. Work with 3 classmates. Say all the lines in the script.

2. Choose your character.

3. Finish the conversation. Write more lines for each character.

4. Practice the lines.

5. Act out the role-play with your group.

Scene 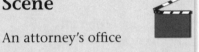	Characters	Props
An attorney's office	• Attorney • Tenant 1 • Tenant 2 • Tenant 3	• Four chairs • A desk

The Script

Attorney: Please sit down. How can I help you?

Tenant 1: We need legal advice.

Attorney: What's the problem?

Tenant 2: Last year, we moved into an apartment.

Tenant 3: Before we moved in, we had to pay a $500 security deposit.

Tenant 1: Two months ago we moved out of the apartment.

Tenant 2: And we were supposed to get the security deposit back.

Tenant 3: We told the landlord to send the check to our new address.

Tenant 1: Unfortunately, he never sent it.

Attorney: Hmm. It might be because there was a problem with the apartment. Did you leave it in good condition?

KEEP GOING!

Watch your classmates' role-plays. Write the answers to these questions: Did the tenants leave the apartment in good condition? Can the attorney help the tenants?

Pair A: Early African American Leaders

1. Find a partner with page 134. You are Pair A.

2. Read the article.

Internet

Address http://www.famousamericans.us   ▾ Go

Before the Civil Rights Movement, African Americans in the U.S. did not have the rights and freedoms that other citizens had. In fact, until 1863, African Americans in the Southern states were slaves. That means they were the property of other people. Some of these slaves became famous for their work to help end slavery. Their amazing stories are an important part of American history.

Harriet Tubman (1820?–1913) was born a slave. At the age of 25, she escaped, or ran away, to the North where there was no slavery. But Tubman was worried about her family members who were still in the South. She decided to go back to help them escape.

This was very dangerous and difficult, but that did not stop Tubman.

After she helped her family escape, Tubman helped another 300 people to freedom with the "Underground Railroad." A railroad is a system of trains and stations that connect towns. The Underground Railroad was a system of houses—the slaves secretly moved from house to house on their way to the North. Tubman became famous for her work. Many people in the South tried to stop her. However, no one ever caught her or any of the people she helped. Tubman was proud to say, "I never ran my train off the track, and I never lost a passenger."

3. Answer the QUESTIONS FOR PAIR A together.

QUESTIONS FOR PAIR A

   a. Why did Harriet Tubman run away to the North?

   _____

   b. Why did she go back to the South?

   _____

   c. What was the Underground Railroad?

   _____

4. Find a Pair B with page 135. Answer their questions about your article.

5. Ask them the QUESTIONS TO ASK PAIR B. Write their answers.

QUESTIONS TO ASK PAIR B

   a. Who taught Douglass to read?

   _____

   b. How did Douglass help end slavery?

   _____

   c. What did Douglass say in one of his famous speeches?

   _____

> **KEEP GOING!**
> Talk about other civil rights leaders. Who else has worked to bring freedom and equal rights to people?

Pair B: Early African American Leaders

1. Find a partner with page 135. You are Pair B.

2. Read the article.

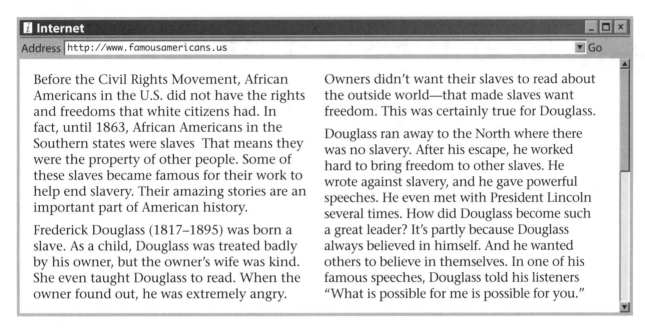

Address http://www.famousamericans.us

Before the Civil Rights Movement, African Americans in the U.S. did not have the rights and freedoms that white citizens had. In fact, until 1863, African Americans in the Southern states were slaves That means they were the property of other people. Some of these slaves became famous for their work to help end slavery. Their amazing stories are an important part of American history.

Frederick Douglass (1817–1895) was born a slave. As a child, Douglass was treated badly by his owner, but the owner's wife was kind. She even taught Douglass to read. When the owner found out, he was extremely angry.

Owners didn't want their slaves to read about the outside world—that made slaves want freedom. This was certainly true for Douglass.

Douglass ran away to the North where there was no slavery. After his escape, he worked hard to bring freedom to other slaves. He wrote against slavery, and he gave powerful speeches. He even met with President Lincoln several times. How did Douglass become such a great leader? It's partly because Douglass always believed in himself. And he wanted others to believe in themselves. In one of his famous speeches, Douglass told his listeners "What is possible for me is possible for you."

3. Answer the QUESTIONS FOR PAIR B together.

QUESTIONS FOR PAIR B

   a. Who taught Douglass to read?

_____

   b. How did Douglass help end slavery?

_____

   c. What did Douglass say in one of his famous speeches?

_____

4. Find a Pair A with page 134. Ask them the QUESTIONS TO ASK PAIR A. Write their answers.

QUESTIONS TO ASK PAIR A

   a. Why did Harriet Tubman run away to the North?

_____

   b. Why did she go back to the South?

_____

   c. What was the Underground Railroad?

_____

5. Answer Pair A's questions about your article.

KEEP GOING!
Talk about other civil rights leaders. Who else has worked to bring freedom and equal rights to people?

Class Election

The Project: Create an election poster
Supplies: poster board, notebook paper, pens, markers, colored pencils or crayons, tape
Resources: dictionaries

1. Work with 3–5 students. Introduce yourself.

2. Choose your job.

   Leader: Help your team work together and watch the time.
   Recorder: Write the team's ideas.
   Supplier: Get the supplies and the resources.
   Graphic Designer: Design the poster.
   Reporter: Tell the class about the project.
   Researcher: Find information to help your team complete the project.

3. Brainstorm answers to these questions: What personal strengths are important in a class president? What skills and experience should a class president have?

   Leader: Give the team 5 minutes. Ask each person the questions.
   Recorder: Write the name and answers of each team member.

4. Choose a candidate and create the poster.

   Supplier: Get the supplies and the resources from your teacher.
   Team:
      • Choose a team member as your candidate for class president.
      • Write about the person's strengths, skills, and experience.
      • Draw a picture of your candidate, or use a photo if available.
   Graphic Designer: Help the team create an attractive poster.
   Researcher: Use a dictionary to help your team with vocabulary and spelling.

5. Show your project to the class.

   Reporter: Show the poster to your classmates and tell them about your candidate.

KEEP GOING!

Have a class election. Write the name of your choice of candidate on a piece of paper, and put the vote in a box. The candidate with the most votes wins!